The Murder of Roseann Quinn

Peter Dover

Published by Richard Poche, 2021.

THE MURDER OF ROSEANN QUINN

First edition. July 4, 2021.

Copyright © 2021 Peter Dover.

ISBN: 979-8224520534

Written by Peter Dover.

THE MURDER OF ROSEANN QUINN

PETER DOVER

When does an enjoyment of varied interests become a double life? That is a question pertinent to the tragic and strange tale of Roseann Quinn. Many will be familiar with this name, even though her death dates back three and a half decades. That is because the case of Roseann Quinn is the one behind the well known 1977 film, 'Looking for Mr Goodbar', which starred Diane Keaton.

It is also the inspiration for Judith Rossner's slightly less well known but still best selling novel of the same name, and the account by the New York Times journalist, Lacey Fosburgh (called 'Closing Time: The True Story of the Goodbar Murder.')

Sometimes, it can be tricky to understand why some crimes make their way to the eye of popular culture and other, equally tragic, events fail to do so. Although, of course, every death is a tragedy for someone. But in the case of Roseann, the answer is clear to see.

Let us spend a moment or two considering what career we might hold up as the epitome of good work, of social benefit. Doctor, nurse, nun? To that list most would add elementary school teacher. But when that educator of the youngest members of our society seeks to specialise in working with the disabled, the neediest of all, then they come closer to sainthood. Roseann was an elementary school teacher, and was developing a specialisation in working with deaf children when she met her untimely death. All of that is enough to warrant a special place for her in the minds of the nation, but take that perfection and flavour it with a taste of a double life, an aspect of living that we would not associate with such a vocation, and our interest is firmly aroused.

Were she alive today, Roseann would have entered deserved retirement from her career. She was born just prior to the end of the Second World War, in 1944. John and her mother, also Roseann, were strongly catholic Irish Americans. The young teacher to be was born in the Bronx, in an aspirational middle class family.

She had three siblings – her two brothers John (the parents liked to pass on the family names) and Dennis. She also had a sister called

Donna. Aged just eleven, Roseann and her family moved out of the Bronx to the rapidly expanding small New Jersey Township of Mine Hill. This was a comfortably middle class, mostly white, Republican small town and perfectly suited the kind of family of which 1950s America boasted. One could almost feel the post war boom in such a community, and the Quinn's (despite their Irish heritage and its associated stereotypes) typified that. John was an executive with the large, nearby organisation Bell Laboratories. All was bright, all was rosy.

The first small blip on the horizon came when Roseann was just thirteen. She developed a condition called scoliosis. With this illness the spine grows in an S shape. It typically affects children as they head through the growth spurts of puberty and is only dangerous in the most serious of cases, where the growth can put pressure on the lungs, resulting in breathing problems. However, in Roseann's case the condition was bad enough to see her spend a year in hospital. But she recovered and headed on to the Morris Catholic High School in Denville, New Jersey.

Her year out did not impact educationally on the quiet, well liked and friendly girl. She graduated successfully and entered teacher training college at the Newark State Teachers College.

The picture is emerging of a young woman who appeared as the opposite of the drug taking, high living, sex fuelled state of twenty somethings we like to picture as symbolic of the 1960s. Following her graduation, this image became even shinier. She gained three years standard teaching experience and then moved into a school for the deaf, working with a class of eight year olds.

She was a popular young teacher, adored by parents and students alike, and respected by her more senior colleagues. Her time was dedicated to her class; she would often stay behind after school supporting them. 'The students loved her,' said a spokesman for her school when news of her death became public. During this time she decided that she wanted to understand more about working with the deaf, and entered into a part time post graduate course.

Slim, attractive and bookish, with large tinted glasses, Roseanne moved into a recently converted apartment in New York. It might not be in the swankiest of homes, but was not a bad way of living for a young, single and poorly paid professional. There she enjoyed a cosmopolitan life. She was the kind of woman who fell easily into company. She had a wide circle of friends, and not just from the world of education. The early part of the 1970s saw the women's movement growing fast. The sexual revolution was underway. If Roseann Quinn bought into this, and it seemed as though she did, then it was in a bookish way. Her carefully decorated West Side studio apartment was not necessarily what might be a typical teacher's home. Nor would this profession be known for sitting alone in bars, drinking wine and reading.

More typical, perhaps, was her diverse circle of friends – artists, professionals, construction workers from all racial groups - she was a true liberal in her attitudes.

It is now that we begin to consider the allegations of a double life which came to prominence following her murder. Perhaps 'double life' is too strong a term. We are in the 1970s, the emancipation of women is speeding up, for a woman steeped in the strongly conservative values of a deeply catholic background, cosmopolitan West side New York must have been like stepping into a kaleidoscope of colour and opportunity.

Yes, Roseann was dedicated, intellectual, sincere. But she was also friendly and, put bluntly, enjoyed the company of the opposite sex. To be single, attractive, in your late twenties and taking full, liberal advantage of that might not have been atypical of her background, but things change. And why not?

It was easy to see why Roseann had not settled down. There were two reasons; her career and her simple enjoyment of a variety of men. A double life? Well, maybe. But that term comes with connotations which are undeserved for a woman who gave so much to her community.

If there is to be a criticism of Roseann Quinn, it is simply that her judgement in choosing the men she led back to the small apartment was not always the best. Perhaps she was attracted to a certain kind of man, perhaps it was simply that this kind of man saw a vulnerability and availability in her. Whichever, neighbours often reported sounds of raised voices and fighting from her apartment. On one occasion, she emerged the next day with a scratched face and a black eye.

Then, on New Year's Day, 1973, tragedy occurred. Roseann followed her regular pattern for when she was not working. In the early evening, she set off by herself to a bar, W M Tweeds, just opposite her home. There, she met with two men – Danny Murray who was a stock broker and his gay lover John Wayne Wilson. The two had been an item for around a year.

To join up with a couple of gay men, back in a time when such behaviour was still frowned upon, was typical of Roseann's liberalism. Indeed, even though the Stonewall riots of a few years back had brought homosexuality into the open, same sex sexual relationships were still, at that time in New York, technically illegal.

When Murray left the bar an hour short of midnight, Roseann and Wilson continued to drink. They decided to head back to her apartment. It was the last time she was seen alive in public.

Three days later her school sent round a teacher to check on their normally highly committed and professional employee. It was completely out of character for her to be absent without informing her employers. Letting down her class and her colleagues was not something with which she was in any way associated. The teacher found the caretaker, and together they went to investigate.

Roseann was dead, murdered and mutilated in horrific fashion. She had been raped and stabbed at least 14 times. She had been beaten on the head using an ornamental metal bust of herself. Bizarrely, a candle had been inserted into her vagina. The apartment was ransacked, and blood spattered the walls. It appeared as though she had been killed in a frenzy of violence.

Police began searching for the last people to see her, and soon identified Murray and Wilson as suspects. But the latter of the two was nowhere to be found. However, Murray quickly admitted that Wilson had confessed the crime to him. He had given his partner cash to travel to his home state of Indiana, where he could stay with his brother.

Within a few days Wilson was arrested and stories of his past began to surface. They were complex to say the least. Wilson was just twenty three years old at the time of his arrest, but in that short life he had married, divorced and fathered two daughters. He had moved from Indiana to Florida, and then on to New York.

Wilson also had a police record, but not one that suggested the kind of violence that had been enacted on Roseann. He had been arrested in Florida on charges of disorder, and served a short spell in prison in Daytona. Then, he had spent time in jail in Kansas on charges of larceny.

In fact, but the time he had hooked up with Murray, he was an escapee from a third prison, this time one in Miami. He had made his way to New York and worked as a street hustler, before joining up with Murray and beginning their sexual partnership. Quite a lot to have achieved by your early twenties.

However, despite his time in prison Wilson was not a hardened criminal; he soon confessed to police his crime, and the murder may well have fallen into the files of the many hideous events that are too numerous to stay in the public's consciousness for long. That was not to be.

Wilson informed the police that he and Roseann were drunk when they arrived back at the fashionable West side apartment. They had moved onto pot: more evidence of Roseann's double life or just the expected behaviour of a single twenty something in the early 70s?

They had fallen into bed – Roseann was eventually discovered on the sofa bed in the apartment's only room – but Wilson had been unable to maintain an erection. He claimed to police that Roseann had taunted him at this point, criticising his sexual performance and mocking his manhood. He had, in the drug and alcohol induced state, suffered a huge and unexpected surge of anger, and had killed his victim in a moment of lost control.

An open and shut case. Or so it should have been, but for another episode which personifies life in the early 1970s. Some would argue it holds true even today. Firstly, once in prison Wilson fell into depression. He was sent for an analysis of his mental and emotional state, which the defence planned to use in mitigation of his crimes. But such considerations were in their infancy back then. Mental health was a cause of amusement and mockery rather than sympathy and understanding. The hospital was small, the psychologists over stretched and underfunded and the priority awarded to a murderer was low in the extreme. Wilson's diagnosis was delayed, then delayed again. In fact, he never reached the stage of seeing a person who may have helped him through his emotional crisis.

Perhaps the State felt that such time and attention was unwarranted. Technically, in 1973 New Jersey still employed the death penalty although in practice nobody had been executed since Ralph Hudson ten years previously. He had been sent to the electric chair after beating his wife to death while on Christmas leave from another sentence he was serving.

Yet there can be little doubt that Wilson was suffering from depression. He was placed on suicide watch, but just as was the case with his psychological analysis, there was a difference between appointment and practice. His New York jail had only a small number of cells in their designated 'suicide watch' section; they were full. There was a long waiting list for them.

So Wilson remained in the main body of the prison. When, one night four months after his arrest, he complained to a guard of his low mood and wish to commit suicide, the guard responded with expected understanding and sympathy.

He offered to supply Wilson with extra sheets so he could use them to hang himself. Indeed, he went further, actually providing the sheets of which Wilson took advantage. Wilson took his own life, and the case was effectively closed.

But that was not the end. However much our modern understanding of the ravaging impacts of mental illness might persuade us towards some sympathy for Wilson, we can still recognise that he was the murderer and Roseann was the victim. It was not the other way round.

That was not how the police appeared to see things, though. Perhaps they were unduly influenced by the tabloid press of the day. And that august body might defend itself by saying it simply reflected the views of the majority of citizens.

The night edition of the New York Daily news for January 5th 1973, a couple of days after Roseann's murder, ran the sensationalist but not hugely controversial headline 'Teacher Victim of Sex Slaying; Battered with Statue of Self'. The juxta position of 'teacher' and 'sex' might raise an eyebrow but otherwise the heading was no more than would be expected from a journal of its kind.

By the time of the final edition, though, the story had taken on a much more lurid twist. 'Teacher Found Nude and Slain' ran the new headline. She was a teacher, and she was nude. Teacher's don't do nude; they wear their underwear in the bath (actually, swimwear, even underwear and pedagogy were incongruous to 1970s America). But if she was a teacher and nude, so the question was raised (in all right thinking people of that enlightened era): didn't she deserve – in part at least – all that she got? The 'Me Too' campaign was still decades away.

But not everybody shared that opinion. Modern women, in particular, refused to see their kind as victims who contributed to their own demise. Over the coming years that viewpoint gained an ever stronger foothold. So the murder and rape of Roseann Quinn became an essential part of the history of the exploitation of women. Exploitation in New York city – in the US as a whole. Indeed, in the entire Western world. Because, in 1973, the rape and murder of a woman is only properly newsworthy if that victim is especially young or especially old – the public can demonstrate suitable outrage at such a crime. Or if she is suitably rich or famous – we all love to read about celebrity. Or, if she is remarkably beautiful.

In a November issue of Time Magazine just a couple of months before Roseann's murder, a former New York City Deputy Police Commissioner had written with disturbing honesty about the police's reaction to serious crime. Robert Daley was speaking before the days when PR experts and political correctness would hide the true values of our major institutions, perhaps making them even more dangerous because of any lack of transparency.

'In New York last year,' he wrote 'we had 1466 murders and many attempted murders. We in the police hierarchy took a personal interest in a few of these: the murder of cops, the Joe Colombo (a contemporary gangster) hit and one or two rape murders distinguished by the youth and beauty of the victim.'

Since we know that rapists consider the beauty of their victims pretty low down their criteria for committing their crime, that the police hierarchy should consider it as paramount is extremely worrying. Or, as might be the case in 1973, extremely normal.

The rape of a beautiful woman sold papers. It sold more if it could be turned into the sort of fantasy certain men might enjoy. And if it became important in the press, so it became important to the police. A very vicious (partly understandable but never justifiable) circle.

And so the murder of Roseann Quinn moved from the merely tragic for her friends and family to one of social importance within the depiction of women by the press, the treatment of women from the police, and the regard of women by (many) men.

If Roseann was found nude, then, goes the thinking, she was egging on her man. If, as Wilson claims, she mocked him for his impotence, then she was entering territory where, well, it is ground from where women are best to stay away. The bedroom is not a banter filled man's locker room but the place where the real business occurs. A man deserves a certain respect. Lead him on, then ridicule him, and frankly (according to the tone sent out by the police over the subsequent months) women deserve what they get.

We might like to think that such misogyny is a thing of the past. But the revelations to emerge from the 'Me Too' campaign suggest that it may not be.

That is perhaps why Roseann's story endures so well today. Yes, being made into a film (or, at least, being the inspiration for one) helps, but does not fully explain why today blogs and articles, TV documentaries and even a rock opera have continued to keep this twenty eight year old teacher's name alive.

Her story illuminates a state of man. Or Woman. Probably both. It could be transferred to Chicago or, with shorts and t shirts replacing the jersey and slacks, to Los Angeles. It could – and does – emerge in London and Paris, Buenos Aires and Tokyo, Shanghai and Lisbon. Hers is the story of individuality subsumed by the machine of social mores. Remember, Roseann is a normal girl. There is little about her that is extra-ordinary when she is viewed from afar. Even the second most abnormal element of her life – behind being murdered – is, in some ways, a sign of her ordinariness. Being hospitalised for a year is unusual, but doesn't everyone have something unusual in their upbringing? It is the absence of abnormality in life that is abnormal.

Of course, when we get into the real person, we see her uniqueness. But the media is not interested in fine detail, it prefers broad brush strokes of vivid, lurid colour. So the 'double life' is created. Teacher versus loner. Worker with the disabled versus sex addict. Or, as we might more properly say, a woman enjoying the new found freedoms of her time.

She heads to the city and makes a life. The life ends in violence and sex, a sordid death with a head bashed in and a vagina stuffed with a candle. It is why, says everybody who celebrates their uniformity, we shouldn't go to the city. Why we shouldn't have one night stands with strangers. Why we should not be alone.

If this were just a story for the 1970s, it would matter less, but it is not.

Leonard Freed, the New York photographer who caught the mood of the seventies better than most, describes an event whereby a young girl stops police to tell them that she has been raped by friends of her boyfriend. He has looked on, and not intervened. As she tells her story, neighbours scream abuse. To speak to the police in that neighbourhood is worse than to be raped. She deserves what she got.

Perhaps the greatest irony of all is that the Goodbar stories take the horror of what happened to Quinn, but then ensure that her life is exaggerated to the extent that sympathy we might hold for a normal woman of her age and time is stretched into voyeurism. The film meant to remember a victim exploits her as much as Wilson, the media, the police.

Her teaching is used merely as a counter balance to her numerous sexual encounters. Not, as in Roseann's real life, as a fundamental (perhaps the most fundamental) part of it. Her sex life is so active that, if true, the real Roseann would have had no time for her further studies, no time to prepare the lessons that made her into the 'much loved' teacher she actually was; certainly no energy to see her through the long, hard days of being a teacher of young deaf children, especially one who commits herself to the well being of her charges well beyond the span of the bells marking the start and end of her days.

But then, if it were to reflect the truth, who would go to see the film? Even when it stars Diane Keaton? Even if she frequently appears in the nude? (A condition allowed in actresses but not in teachers, it would seem). Certainly the audience for such a film would more likely consist of the donnish sociology types than those after either social or sexual titillation. And there are less of the intellectuals. Fewer bums on seats. Smaller takings at the box office. Such a film would not, either, be likely to draw an actor with the pulling power of Richard Gere.

So a tragic death in horrific circumstances is used as the starting point for a film fundamentally about a sexy teacher (and who doesn't like one of those? No doubt Freud could pin point some biological need satisfied by the provision of school milk by our kindergarten mistresses). In its way, a piece of cinema alleging to be a celebration of a life and the eulogy to a death are as exploitative as the men who beat and, eventually, kill the Roseanns, and the hundreds like her across the city, the country, the world.

Incidentally, in Rossner's novel (and the subsequent film) the eponymous Goodbar is the (unsubtle) name of the bar which, in real life, was W M Tweedy.

We cannot escape the unwitting role Roseann has played in the development of the rights of women over the last forty five years. Maybe, she looks down proudly, if a little sadly for all she has had to abandon in becoming the poster girl for women's rights. The feminist writer Susan Brownmiller analysed how victims of rape are presented in the tabloid press. If they are beautiful, then it is in a way that allows men to fantasise over their victimhood. If they are not, then they are hardly reported, unless some other sensationalist idea can be developed to sell the story.

The message is worrying on many levels. It suggests that all men are prone to violence and sexual aggression. Hopefully, only the minority of narrow thinkers would support that notion today, but the rise of internet pornography, the continued stories of sexual exploitation suggest that, if not the norm, then the condition is at least wide spread.

In his Nobel Prize winning novel 'Lord of the Flies' the author William Golding writes about the 'darkness of man's heart.' It is a powerful line; Golding could be referring to man in the widest sense of human life, or simply the male species. It is difficult to be sure. The book itself has no female characters. Even the protagonist, Ralph, speaks more about his Father (capital deliberate) than his mother (lower case equally deliberate). The only female to merit any attention is Piggy's overpowering Aunt. As the name suggest, Piggy becomes a victim in the dystopian story. The novel is devoid of sex – it was written in the 1950s and features twelve year old boys from (Piggy apart) England's most prestigious schools, so any notion of sex is properly avoided – but is full of violence. The message Golding conveys is clear. Despite any advantages we might have in life, our overriding motivation is violence. For adults, we may add the words 'and sex'.

At least, that is the message to which the tabloid press has played. And, the police to whom the attractiveness of a victim determines the attention given to the crime. Also to the film industry, for whom sensationalism always out paces reality.

Maybe times are changing. Maybe not. Sexual predators still exist. Broad stroke views of what is acceptable and what is not might be different, but are still as simplistic. The implication in 1973 might have been that Roseann Quinn got what she deserved because she was a teacher who liked to have sex with men. That would probably hold little weight today. But try suggesting the opposite. Post on social media a view that is not in the increasingly narrow list of what is politically right on, such as that a person might, for whatever reason, make a false accusation and ruin a man (or woman's) life. Do so and the full weight of Facebook will descend upon your head. You will be blocked as readily as Roseann was blamed.

However, for all the associations of her case, it is with Roseann Quinn that we should end. In a way she was a victim who became a cause. A just cause, but one nevertheless. If a person comes to inspire a crusade then their own personal characteristics are easily lost. They become washed in the tide of progress. And lost in it. We should never forget that, more than anything else, Roseann Quinn was a great teacher.

And an undeserving victim

MANSON GIRL : THE TRUE STORY OF RUTH ANN MOOREHOUSE

15

BELINDA WEIDLIN

15

As the trial of Charles Manson gripped a nation, the stories of those whose lives he had touched also fell into the media spotlight. Many of these were the 'girls' in the Family, often referred to as Manson's girls. And of these girls, there was one by far that received the most attention and has maintained this in the form of an unwanted cult following: Ruth Ann Moorehouse. Ruth joined the Family very early on in her life, which led to a string of events that would plague the rest of her life.

Dean Moorehouse was born in 1920 in Minnesota and grew up in Minneapolis with at least two older siblings. When he was 19 years old, he married Audrey Lucile Sirpless and the two proceeded to have four children. Kathlees Adair, their first child was born the year after they were married. Deane Thomas was born the year after that. In 1945, Sharon Lee was born, and the youngest of the siblings Ruth was born in 1951. While all of Ruth's siblings were born in America, she was born in Toronto, Canada, leading to theories that she is not the biological daughter of Dean and Audrey Moorehouse. Another contributing factor to this theory is that different resources list Ruth as having been born in 1951, 1952, and 1953. However, there is no solid evidence to support the claim that she is adopted, and much of it is centered around a two minute conversation with a reporter recorded many years later where Manson rambles about Ruth being an adopted Indian woman who he rescued from a horrible family life.

In 1967, when Dean and his family met Charlie, he was either currently or formerly employed as a Protestant minister. In his autobiography, Charles Manson recounts the time when he first met Dean Moorehouse when Charles was a young, hitchhiking ex-con:

> "I was headed south and a heavy, bald-headed guy gave me a
> ride in his pickup truck. He was kind of a religious fanatic,
> so naturally he wanted to save my soul. By the time we got
> to where he had to turn off he had decided I should share
> dinner with him and his family. Being hungry and having no

schedule to keep, I figured, what the hell, I could listen to his preaching for a while."

And this is how Charlie Manson first met Ruth Moorehouse. Charlie had also been travelling with two girls at the time, Lynette Fromme and Mary Brunner. Manson, Fromme, and Brunner all stayed for dinner and ended up staying the night. Much of the night was spent singing religious songs, whereupon Charlie admired the family piano. Dean told Charlie that he was welcome to have the piano, and to come back to their residence at any time. Charlie remembers his fondness for the instrument, and also another thing that he had laid his eyes on.

"I left with an invitation to revisit his home any time I was in the area. More importantly, because I had admired their piano the night before, he told me the piano was mine if I wanted it. He may have thought I'd never be in the area again to claim the gift, but I very much wanted that piano. I had another reason for returning: he has a beautiful young daughter, and by the looks I was getting she was just as interested in me."

Manson visited the Manson house frequently during that summer, and his company was welcomed by all members of the household aside from Audrey. During those summer months, Charlie laid eyes on a Volkswagen van in the driveway of another resident of San Jose. Having not owned a set of wheels since he had been incarcerated, he describes seeing the van as somewhat like falling in love. He knew that he had to have it, but had less than thirty dollars to his name. Then, he thought of the Moorehouse family piano.

Charlie walked up to the front door of the man who owned the Volkswagen van and began to strike up a deal. Eventually, it was agreed that if he delivered the piano to the man's door then he could have the van. Charlie went and explained the situation to Dean, who gave him the piano and even used his pickup truck to transport it. Charlie was in love.

> "The van was not only transportation, it was a home on wheels that afforded me a nomadic lifestyle. Those first weeks in my new van were among the happiest of my entire life. Mary and I fixed it up so that it was a regular little whorehouse on wheels. I don't mean broads were turning tricks in it, but it was a love pad. It was no problem to stop anywhere, with anyone, and make love for a few minutes, hours, or even days if I wanted to."

Unfortunately for Audrey and Dean Moorehouse, this was not their final interaction with Charlie. Even as he said goodbye and drove away with Fromme and Brunner, he had already made plans with fourteen year old Ruth Ann to meet him a day later and drive with them to Mendocino. Charlie describes this time in a very mixed manner, but summarizes it as "the most memorable and rewarding experience of my life."

On the way to Mendocino, Charlie recalls feeling like he and Ruth Ann had somewhat of a father-daughter relationship. He notes that as he drove she was full of curiosity and wonder, asking him questions about almost anything that her eyes fell on. He answered her questions as much as he was able, and delighted in how thrilled she was with the world. Thrilled she seemed just to be alive. When they got out at the beach, she ran barefoot in the sand and Charlie remembers that he "admired the beauty of her body and her youthful energy as she chased the out-going waves." After she was done playing on the beach, he recalls that it "felt natural" to go inside the van and dry off. He began kissing her lightly and moved to having his hand on her breast. Charlie recalls that she did not struggle, and that she seemed to want him as much as he wanted her. "I treated her like the most delicate flower on earth", he states. The only time that be remembers any resistance was when he moved to take off her underwear, to which she said "But my daddy...". Charlie Manson responded "Forget your daddy. I'm your daddy. Doesn't this feel too good to be wrong?" She didn't provide any resistance after that, and Charlie speaks off feeling "gratified for taking a gift that was denied me in my youth".

When Charlie made this comment, it is likely that he was referring to his stint in a boy's boarding school when he was younger where he claims to have been repeatedly raped. Charlie's mother, Kathleen Maddox, was sixteen when she had Charlie. She was imprisoned when he was very young, and he was sent to live with family where they struggled with his often violent and threatening tendencies. When Kathleen was released and Charlie was put in her care, she found it difficult to cope. The woman who had traded her baby for a pitcher of beer when he was a newborn sent him off to boarding school and wouldn't allow him to come home, even when he escaped and turned up at her door begging. While there has never been any evidence that Manson was raped during his time at school, he is adamant that this happened to him over the course of several years.

When he first had intercourse with Ruth Ann, Manson recalls totally forgetting the age difference between them – Ruth Ann being fourteen and Charlie thirty-two at this stage. He remembers feeling like he was sixteen and having sex with somebody for the first time, despite being divorced and having had many girl friends and hook ups. Looking back, Charlie claims "that thirty minutes of passion in the arms of a fourteen-year-old girl put me a little bit closer to liking a world I had hated since the very early years of my life."

During the trip to Mendocino, Ruth Ann's parents had reported her as a runaway. The cops tracked down Manson and he was arrested when he attempted to convince the police that they didn't need to take Ruth Ann back and that she wasn't happy at home. Ruth Ann was returned to her parents and placed on probation.

"Dean and his wife came to get their daughter and I was put on the good preacher's "don't come around" list. But when a guy wants something, he doesn't follow the rules. When I thought about moving permanently to L.A., I realized I wasn't above looking into the mouth of the lion if there was a possibility of stealing away the young cub."

When Manson was released, he immediately began plotting a way to steal Ruth away for good. Driving around in the Microbus, he had picked up many followers, most of them girls. He drove the bus full of young people to the Moorehouse's door banking on the fact that Dean wouldn't be able to resist preaching to such a wide audience and potentially saving the souls of at least a few of these wayward travelers. Dean began preaching, and everything started to go according to Charlie's plan. What Dean didn't know was that Pat, Mary, Lyn, and Susan were "well-versed in the Bible", and that they had developed their own ideas on the concepts within it. Not only did the Reverend have to be extremely careful because they would pick up on his slightest misquotation, but they bombarded him with counter-argument after count-argument until he became quite frazzled and confused. However, Dean persisted in his attempt to bring the bus-load of young people to the light. While this was happening, the next phase of the plan was being put into play.

"At the time, I'd have liked nothing better than to tell Ruth Ann to get her things ready and leave with us, which is what she wanted to do, but she was still just fourteen and already on probation for running away. Taking her with us would have been inviting police trouble. Instead, I told her, 'We're going to southern California, so we won't be seeing you for a while."

Ruth Ann burst into tears and said that she wanted to leave with the group immediately, but Charlie explained that this would create too much trouble for everyone. Lyn came over and also talked with Ruth. She explained that, due to her age, Ruth had to do anything that her parents saw fit. However, if she were to get married then she would be able to do anything she liked after that point.

Due to the presence of these guests and various other stresses in the marriage, Audrey left the family home at this point to go and live with her mother while she filed for divorce. One night, Ruth Ann broke down in front of her father saying "Daddy, I love Charlie. We made love together and I want to be with him." Dean, in a rampage, left San Jose and tracked down the Microbus to an acid pad in L.A. Dean had brought a friend with him who, upon entering the room, directed a pistol at Charlie's head. He proceeded to tell Charlie what a "rotten, child-raping bastard" he was. Charlie assessed the situation, asked one of his girls to get the two men soft drinks, and allowed Dean to continue berating him while his friend had the pistol pointed at Charlie. When Dean had calmed down somewhat, Charlie launched into a plan that he had been hatching while Den spoke.

Charlie claimed that the business was between the two of them, and that Dean's friend should go for a walk and let just the two of them sort it out like men. Dean agreed, and when his friend had left Charlie offered him a pill that he claimed would bring bean's blood pressure down. Dean accepted the pill, which unbeknownst to him contained a hit of acid. Dean continued to rant at Charlie, and Charlie allowed this as he watched the acid begin to take effect. He then launched into a speech where he attempted to win over the Reverend and lay the foundations for Ruth coming to be a part of the Family.

"Look, Reverend, it ain't like I did something nasty to your little girl. I only did what goes through your mind every time you look at a pretty girl. Now you're a preacher, so you know it's just as evil to lust for something as to do it. Hey, I only did what you would like to do. And you can't blame me or that girl. If you'd spend more time paying attention to your family and doing what you preach to everyone else, that girl wouldn't be looking for some way to get out of your house. Man, don't you see, with all your religious convictions, you're not giving your daughter a chance to live her own life. Kids grow up fast these days. They got to have space. Space that ain't smothered by parents who are locked into yesterday."

Dean left without further argument, and got into his friend's car. A couple of weeks later he returned to see Charlie, but it wasn't anything to do with Ruth Ann. He wanted acid from Manson, and to "join a world he had always preached against". During this time, two things happened. Ruth Ann married a bus driver and left him one day later, now emancipated from her family and free to travel to California to be with Charlie. She was now Ruth Heuvelhorst, but she soon dropped her name all together. While Ruth Ann was figuring out how to get back to Charlie, her father got arrested twice for drug possession and trafficking. In the first instance, Dean was arrested and charged with contributing to the delinquency of a minor during a marijuana raid in a Redwood Valley home. A couple of months later, Dean was arrested once more, this time from a tipoff from Roger Tholan and Gertrude Romanski that the fifty dollars worth of acid that they were caught in possession of had been sold to them by Dean. Dean made one more attempt to get Ruth Ann back by finding Charlie at Dennis Wilson's house (of the 60s band the Beach Boys), but Charlie welcomed the preacher by kissing his feet and welcoming him to the party. As he awaited trail in the house, he made no more attempts to remove Ruth Ann from the situation, becoming a devout follow of Charlie's and pushing his lifestyle and philosophy on anybody that would talk to him. He then travelled to Spahn Ranch to connect with other members of the Family, and where his little girl had begun to distance herself from the name of Ruth Ann and adopt the name of Ouish. He was found guilty in December of 1968 and sent to prison.

It was from this time that Ruth began to hold a significant place in the Family. While she and Charlie both claim that all of the girls and men were shared and loved equally, it is clear from a variety of accounts that Ouish was the favorite of not only Charlie, but many of the other men. Somebody who particularly favored her was Terry Melcher, the son of Doris Day who was a music produced that had been introduced to Charles Manson by Dennis Wilson. At the ranch, Manson would ask his girls to entertain the men to increase his favor with them. While Manson's girls insist that they always did this of their own free will, there was still a degree that Manson had some control over them. When she wasn't entertaining people who had come to the ranch, Ouish spent a lot of time helping out the Family with various household tasks. She would go dumpster diving with others so that they could have fruit and vegetables without needing to pay for them. Much of her time was spent looking after the babies and young children on the farm, as everything was done as a community. However, Ouish's life was about to be turned upside down.

In August of 1969, a week after the Tate murders, Ruth Ann was arrested with the rest of the Family during the Spahn's Ranch raid. She was also arrested in October at the Barker Ranch raid and is quoted as saying "Just before we got busted in the desert, there was twelve of us apostles and Charlie." That year she had two interviews with the LAPD in December and a Grand Jury Testimony in the same month. Throughout all of these interactions, Ouish remained loyal to the family and attempted to answer all questions in the most vague manner possible without angering the authority figures that she was interacting with. She was seventeen at the time, and speaks about taking acid and her Family members. She claimed that she had only heard about the Tate murders on the radio and the television, and that there had been no discussion about it on the ranch. Ouish later told Barbara Hoyt that she knew of ten more murders that had occurred other than Sharon Tate, but did not seem phased by this. When she was released from jail, she briefly went to live with her mother and attended high school for the first time. However, she went back to the Family. Ruth Ann, Fromme, Sandra Good, Catherine Gillies, Nancy Pitman and other members of the Family would camp outside of the courthouse during the trials in an attempt to defend Manson and the other members of the Family who had been incarcerated. This is when the girls carved and burned the X of their foreheads to show their support for Manson. It was not that Ruth Ann was part of a plan to stop Barbara Hoyt from testifying that shaped and ruined the rest of Ruth Ann's life.

Barbara Hoyt, who was born in 1951, started living with the Family in April of 1969. On the night of the Tate murders, Hoyt was asked to collect three sets of black clothes by Susan Atkins. She observed the reaction of the Family to the Tate murders over the next few days and became suspicious. She was arrested and released in August alongside Ouish and the other members of the Family, and she awoke to the screams of Donald Shea as Family members killed him one week later. In Death Valley, Hoyt and another of Manson's girls Sherry Cooper overheard Susan Atkins say to Ruth Ann that she had killed Sharon Tate. Hoyt and Cooper fled from the Family. Manson caught up with the pair in a dinner in the town of Ballarat, and gave the girls enough money to get to L.A. However, there are also claims that Manson then later sent three members of the Family to either retrieve or kill the girls.

In 1970, Hoyt was still undecided as to whether she wanted to testify in the Tate/Labianca murder trial. Manson took advantage of her indecision and offered to send Hoyt on an all expenses paid trip to Hawaii with Ouish. On the 9th September, Ouish made a phone call and said that she had to return and eave Hoyt by herself. She gave Hoyt a burger which was laced with ten hits of acid and went to catch her flight. As the drug began to take effect, Hoyt ran screaming out onto the sidewalk and collapsed. A passerby took Hoyt to the emergency room an Hoyt's mother came to take her back home. It was then clear in Hoyt's mind that she would testify in the Tate/Labianca case.

Ruth Ann and several other family members associated with the Hawaiian Hamburger episode were sought after on charges of Conspiracy to Prevent and Dissuade a Witness, and Conspiracy to Commit Murder. When Ruth was arrested in December, the latter charge had been dropped. She was released, and all five members of the Family associated with the incident were to serve ninety days in prison. However, Ruth Ann was not nine months pregnant and refused to have her baby in jail. The Family gave her orders to shave off her hair and give birth to the baby in prison, but she instead fled to Carson City in Nevada to live with her sister where she had her baby four days later. The D.A.'s office felt that it was too much trouble to extradite her and Ruth Ann never served the ninety days.

After this time, Ruth Ann married a builder from Reno and had another child. She then moved to Sacramento but made no connections with Family members Fromme and Good who lived in the same city. Fromme and Good had made repeated calls to Ruth Ann's sister's house trying to get back in contact with Ouish and bring her back into the fold. She later married again, and now lives with her three children in the Mid-west trying to keep as much of a low profile as she can. Ruth Ann has had the X on her forehead surgically removed, but she still finds it impossible to integrate fully with others and lead a normal life. While she does have friends, she is unable to talk about that period in her life with them. Furthermore, as so many of her foundational years were spent in the Family, she had no stories of growing up, going to school, and being a teenager. She raised her children telling them that she lived in a commune, but not that she had anything to do with the Family.

Probably the most significant correspondence with the public that Ruth Ann has made since the trials is a letter to Bill Nelson who kept up a now defunct website called mansonmurders.com. Ruth Ann, who had read the website page about herself, thanked him for not releasing further information and wanted to tell her story of her more recent life. While her behavior cannot be excused simply because of her age or situation, the following letters gives us some insight into the horrors that Ruth Ann has experienced due to her time that she spent with the Family as one of Manson's girls. The time when she was a girl called Ouish.

I have been living a quiet life for the past 30 years. I have been blessed well beyond what I have deserved. I have a great husband who I adore, a job I love, and sons who are my whole being. But there have been many tragedies along the way. I am not trying to make anyone feel sorry for me, I am merely trying to "set the stage" for what has become of my life.

I received my first email from Bill back in July. I admit that it hit me out of the blue. I had seen his website and had also seen him interviewed on television. I didn't know what to expect. I hadn't talked about those years of my life for a long, long time. Indeed, my own children don't know my history. I have been up front with them about the drug use and basically told them I lived in a "commune". They have no idea I was with Manson.

I tried to explain to Bill my reluctance to "speak out" because it had been so long. I have been living quietly with this for almost thirty years. Old habits are hard to break. For a moment put yourself in my shoes. Have you ever tried to explain to a plastic surgeon why you have an 'X' on your forehead in the first place? I have had all these feelings bottled up tight for many years. I have been to professional counseling for years. I can't talk to my friends about it. Real friends will understand? Wrong! I know from firsthand experience that is not the case. I have tried "opening up" before and have had people (special people) walk out of my life because of it. Welcome to my life.

I told Bill this story. I live in a VERY small town. One cold night, I couldn't sleep. I flipped on the TV and there happened to be a Sharon Tate movie (DON'T MAKE WAVES) showing. I cried the rest of the night. I think about it all the time. Not a day goes by when I don't think back wishing the whole thing was some awful dream. But it wasn't a dream. I know that. I can't change it, although I would if I could.

Barbara Hoyt. I think about her and wish that there was something I could do to ease her pain. What I did was despicable. I am ashamed. But again, I can't take back something I did 30 years ago. The reason I never apologized to Barbara through email to Bill is quite simple. I can't fully express my feelings in words. I feel it is something that needs to be done face to face. At this time however, Bill has told me that Barbara doesn't want some type of overly emotional reunion to be blasted all over the talk shows. I feel the same way. Like I said, I think about Barbara on a daily basis. What happened with her has kept me up nights for 30 years thinking about what could have been a very tragic outcome. I am truly sorry.

After reading Bill's website update about me, I felt compelled to give my side of the story. Bill has been getting a bad rap on the message boards and I probably shouldn't have "popped off" the way I did. As far as I know, he hasn't spilled any information about me. Basically, everything happened too fast for me. Much too fast. I wanted to set the record straight and give insight into my decision to do what I did.

THE BEAUMONT CHILDREN

BARBARA DUKE

It was a warm summer morning on January 26, 1966, when the three Beaumont children left their suburban home to celebrate Australia Day at the beach. The children regularly made the trip by themselves, so their mother felt at ease providing them with bus fare and sending them on their way while she visited and had lunch with a close friend. However, she would return home that afternoon to find that the children still had not returned. That morning would end up being the last time she saw her three children.

Jane (aged 9), Arnna (aged 7), and Grant (aged 4), lived in Somerton Park, a quiet suburb minutes away from Adelaide, South Australia. Their father, Jim Beaumont, was a linen goods salesman who frequently traveled for work and their mother, Nancy Beaumont, was a stay-at-home mother.

The oldest child, Jane, was viewed by her parents as responsible enough to supervise the other children for short trips and adventures, a style of parenting that was the norm in Australia at that time. The children frequently took the five-minute bus ride to neighboring Glenely Beach by themselves and were looking forward to celebrating the national holiday at the beach.

The children left their home at 10:00am that morning and were seen arriving at the beach by witnesses at 10:15am. They spent much of that morning at play on the beach and were supposed to arrive home at 2:00pm. When they did not arrive at the appointed time, their mother assumed that they had become preoccupied with celebrating the holiday with their playmates and that they would arrive on the next bus or had decided to walk home, something that the three children had done before. When the children did not disembark from the next scheduled bus, their mother began to grow worried.

The disappearance of the Beaumont children would result in one of the largest manhunts and police investigations in Australian history. Furthermore, the event had widespread consequences on Australian society, shattering the illusion that many parents had regarding their children's safety and changing the way that Australians parented their children forever.

Timeline of Events

10:00am - The children leave their Somerton Park home to travel to Glenely Beach by bus.

10:15am - They are seen exiting the bus by multiple witnesses.

11:00am - The three children are spotted playing beneath a sprinkler by an elderly woman. A tall blond man is spotted lying on the ground next to them, watching the children play.

11:15am - A tall blond man is seen playing with the children. They all appear to be laughing and at ease.

11:45am - The children purchase several pastries and a meat pie from the beach snack shop.

12:15pm - The tall blond man and the children are seen leaving the beach together. The children are witnessed laughing together and holding hands.

3:00pm - A postman on his route spots the children walking along Jetty Road alone, away from the beach. The postman is known to the children and they exchange greetings. Police believe that the timeline for this event is incorrect.

7:20pm - The parents of the children become gravely concerned and file a missing children's report with the local police department. Jim Beaumont and the local police search the entire Glenely Beach area.

8:40pm - Police search the surrounding beaches with no results. The father contacts friends and relatives in an attempt to locate the children.

10:00pm - Police issue public radio announcements with a missing children report.

Points of Interest

There are several details in this story which raised doubts with both the parents of the children and the local police department. When the children departed for Glenely Beach in the morning of January 26th, they left with only enough money to cover their bus fare: six shilling and a sixpence. However, the shop owner, who sold several pastries and a meat pie to the children at 11:45am, reported that the children paid for the food with a $1 bill, an amount of money that they did not have when they left their mother's care.

In addition, the shop owner knew the children well and had sold them food and pastries several times before. He reported that the children had never purchased a meat pie before. This suggests that the children received the money from someone after leaving their parents home and that they may have been purchasing the meat pie for someone else.

Lastly, the mother of the children, Nancy Beaumont, repeatedly said that her children were quite shy and very unlikely to speak with strangers, indicating that they may have met the tall blond man prior to the date of their disappearance. Their mother also remembered a seemingly innocuous comment from Arnna, who had previously told her mother that Jane had "got a boyfriend down the beach." Nancy assumed that her daughter was referring to a young playmate, but in hindsight it seems that she may have been referring to the tall blond man spotted by witnesses.

Police Investigation

The South Australian police force began investigating the disappearance of the children in full-force the evening of their disappearance. After interviewing several witnesses who were present at Glenely Beach, they were able to determine that the children were playing with a tall blond, "thin-faced" man while at the beach. He was described as being a blond man in his late 30s with a thin or athletic build.

"Things seemed bungled from the get-go," forensic psychologist Paula Orange said. "First off, the artist drawing the picture admitted to being drunk at the time of completing his task. So the sketch made of the suspect looks more like a lantern-jawed alien than a real person. Secondly, the witnesses claimed that the man was in his late thirties. Witnesses are notorious for getting ages wrong and the police dismissed too many possible subjects out of hand because they didn't fit the profile."

Several witnesses stated that the man was seen dressing the children prior to leaving the beach. The children's parents said that the kids, especially Jane, were very shy and unlikely to speak to a stranger. This later led police to theorize that the children had met the man in question prior to the date of their disappearance and had grown to know him over a period of several weeks.

The blond man and three children were seen leaving the beach together at 12:15pm, after the children purchased several pastries and a meat pie from a local vendor with a $1 bill, an amount of money that they did not have when they left their home that morning.

A wrench was thrown into the investigation when a postman, who knew the children and was on friendly terms with them, reported that he saw the children around 3:00pm that afternoon walking away from the beach and in the direction of their home in Somerton Park. He stated that he exchanged greetings with the young children and that they seemed to be in good spirits. In particular, the postman said that he say the children were "holding hands and laughing" as they walked down the road alone, with no blond companion in sight. Police later said that they believed the postman was mistaken about the timeline and that he most likely saw the children walking some time before noon.

Several months later, a woman in a nearby neighborhood contacted police and told them that she had seen a man with two girls and a young boy enter an abandoned house on her street. She also reported seeing the young boy walking away from the house before he was roughly grabbed by, and returned to the house with, the older man. She never saw the man or children again.

"The response from the public was overwhelming," Orange said. "People drove from miles away to aid in the search. They combed the beach and drained part of it all to no avail. They found nothing, not a trace."

The police were quickly able to eliminate drowning as the cause of the children's disappearance as a result of several witnesses saying that they saw the children leave the beach around 12:15pm. Furthermore, all of the children's belongings were missing, lending further support to the theory that they left the beach. After speaking with the parents, the police were able to identify seventeen different items that were carried by the children that day, providing a list of items that could be used to identify their remains or whereabouts. However, the police's continue efforts continued to prove fruitless.

The Psychic Circus

On November 8, 1966, nearly a year after the children's initial disappearance, an internationally-renowned psychic from the Netherlands, Gerard Croiset, was flown to Australia to investigate the case. His presence caused a whirlwind of media coverage in Australia and across the world. After making a series of outlandish and ever-changing claims, Croiset claimed that the children were buried underneath a warehouse just minutes away from the children's school.

"I appreciate him (Gerard Croiset) coming out to find the children," Jim Beaumont said. "But I don't believe what he said. I don't believe the children are dead and will continue to believe until given evidence that proves otherwise."

The building, which was under construction at the time of their disappearance, was eventually razed and excavated after the owners raised $40,000 for the project as a result of public pressure. No evidence of the children or their belongings were ever found.

"The press and police followed Croiset around everywhere," Orange said. "He was an obvious con artist but they were desperate. They had nothing."

A Series of Letters

Beginning in 1968, the parents of the three children began to receive a series of letters which rekindled hope in the idea that their children may still be alive. Postmarked from Dandernong, Victoria, the series of letters claimed to be written by Jane, the eldest daughter. She claimed to be under the supervision of a man and in good health and care, saying

Dear Mum and Dad,

We had a beautiful lunch today…The man is feeding us really well. The man took us to see The Sound of Music yesterday.

Police officers believed the letters to be from Jane after comparing them to examples of her handwriting and, as far as 1981, the Sidney Morning Herald produced analysis from handwriting experts claiming that the letters were actually from the missing child.

Following receipt of the letters supposedly sent from Jane, the parents received a letter from a man claiming to be in possession of the children. He said that he was willing to hand the children over to the parents at a specific time and location. The Beaumonts arrived at the appointed time and location with an undercover police officer but no one showed. They later received a letter from the same man claiming that he saw the undercover police officer arrive with the parents and that he would now keep the children, ending any hope of a peaceful exchange.

In 1992, following another investigation and remarkable achievements in fingerprint technology, authorities identified the author of the letters as a local man who was just a teenager at the time of the hoax. He reportedly wrote and mailed the letters as "a joke."

False Closure

Then, in November 2013, South Australian police received an anonymous tip claiming that the children were buried underneath a warehouse located in North Plympton. Although radar identified "one small anomaly, which can indicate movement or objects within the soil," no evidence was ever found.

The Suspects

Bevan Spencer von Einem

Bevan Spencer von Einem has long been considered the prime suspect in the disappearance of the Beaumont children. Einem was convicted of the July 1983 murder of fifteen-year-old Richard Kelvin, son of a popular news reporter, in 1984. Police have long suspected Einem of working with a series of accomplices and of having committed other abductions and murders.

In 1983, a police informant known as "Mr. B" told police that Einem claimed to have taken three children from a beach to perform medical "experiments," claiming that he performed "brilliant surgery" on the three children before accidentally killing one of them. Following the child's accidental death, the informant stated that Einem claimed to have killed the other two children and buried them in an open field outside the city of Adelaide.

Einem did bare some resemblance to the descriptions of the tall blond man given to police following the disappearance of the Beaumont children and was known to frequent Glenely Beach to spy on people in the changing rooms. He was also noted as having an obsession with children.

Einem worked as an accountant and lived with his mother. There were rumors that he was part of a ring of Adelaide professionals who shared a "hobby" of kidnapping, drugging and raping boys.

"Einem did match the description of the police sketches," Orange said. "And he did like to frequent the same beach. He seemed more interested in young teenage males as his list of known victims would indicate. Einem was a homosexual who picked up hitchhikers with his transvestite friend where they would engage in a "rough trade" style of sex. He would take photographs of his victims as a keepsake. The three young children would seem to be outside of his modus operandi."

However, Einem was significantly younger than the suspect described by witnesses; Einem was around 20 years old at the time, while the description of the suspect placed him in his late 20s. But, in 2007 local police officers identified a young man who looked exactly like a young Einem in Channel 7 news footage of the incident taken days after the disappearance. He remains a prime suspect in the case.

"The newly found news footage does implicate Einem in a psychological way," Orange said. "Killers often like to return to the scene of the crime. He was spotted on film, days after the disappearance. What are the odds against that?"

Arthur Stanley Brown

Arthur Stanley Brown, along with Einem, is considered to be one of two prime suspects in the abduction of the Beaumont children. In 1988, Brown, then 86 years old, was charged with kidnapping, raping, and murdering Judith and Susan Mackey in Townsville, Queensland. His first trial was declared a mistrial after the jury failed to reach a verdict in the case and his second trial was blocked because he was declared unfit to stand trial; Brown was suffering from dementia and Alzheimer's disease by this time.

He is considered one of two prime suspects in the case because of his connection to the murder of other children and because of his remarkable resemblance to descriptions of the tall blond man seen with the children at the time of their disappearance. He was also a prime suspect in the Adelaide Oval case, which involved the disappearance of Joanna Ratcliffe and Kirste Gordon.

"Brown was a known pedophile by his closest family members," Orange said. "He is alleged to have molested numerous younger relatives. He could be placed in the same area and time of the Beaumont children but nothing could be proven."

Although Brown is considered to be a prime suspect in the disappearance of the Beaumont children, the suspect in the case was identified as being in his late 30s; Brown was in his 50s at the time. Brown died in 2002 without ever admitting to the crime.

"Brown would move into a nursing home at the end of his life," Orange said. "He would die an innocent man with the courts never able to officially charge him because of his Alzheimer's."

James Ryan O'Neill

James Ryan O'Neill, convicted of murdering nine-year-old Ricky John Smith in the Australian state of Tasmania in 1975 and currently serving a life sentence for the crime, was considered as a suspect in the Beaumont children disappearance for some time. He is reported as having told several friends in the early 1970s that he was responsible for the disappearance of the Beaumont children in 1966. However, he was publicly eliminated as a suspect by the South Australian police. He remains in prison in Tasmania to this day.

"O'Neill was the subject of a documentary called 'The Fishermen," Orange said. "In the documentary, he is evasive about being the man behind the disappearance of the children. He is, however, at the forefront of most pundits who have studied the story. While Brown and Einem did not have charming personas, O'Neill did. He was handsome and smiley with the ability to manipulate everyone around him. He could fabricate lies at the drop of a hat so it is easy to believe that he would be able to charm the children into his acquaintance. People who knew him all described him as 'the most likable man you'll ever meet.' No one could believe that he would be capable of such an act."

Derek Ernest Percy

In 2007, the Victorian newspaper The Age published a report stating that Derek Ernest Percy, at the time the longest-serving prisoner in the southeastern Australian state, was responsible for the disappearance of the Beaumont children in 1966. Initially jailed in

1970 for the 1969 murder of 12-year-old Yvonne Tuohy, Percy was found not guilty of the crime by reason of insanity, but was nonetheless jailed "indefinitely."

He is widely considered to be Australia's worst child serial killer and is suspected of the killings of the Beaumont children, as well as the abduction, attempted rape, and stabbing of Marianne Schmidt and Christine Sharrock on January 11, 1965. In October 2014, Percy was also ruled to have abducted and killed seven-year-old Linda Stilwell in 1968. However, Percy passed away from cancer in 2013, having never admitted to any of his crimes. He remains a possible suspect in the case.

"Percy is unique in that he may have had his mother not aiding him but covering up for him," Orange said. "He is certainly one of the most sadistic pedophiles on record, his doings are unmentionable out of respect for his victims. He was in the city at the time of the Beaumont children disappearance and is probably the top suspect along with O'Neill. His mother, however, has thrown out a lot of what could have been evidence in the case."

Related Cases

Two similar cases to the disappearance of the Beaumont children attracted widespread attention in the South Australian media, and the primary suspect in the Beaumont children's kidnapping case was convicted in one case and suspected in the other.

The Adelaide Oval Case

On August 25, 1972, two young girls, Joanne Ratcliffe (aged 11) and Kirste Gordon (aged 4) went missing while attending an Australian football game. They are presumed dead. This case also received widespread attention in the South Australian media and Bevan Spencer von Einem was considered the primary suspect in their disappearance.

Einem matched the descriptions of the tall blond man provided by witnesses in the Beaumont children's case and closely resembles the police sketch released to the public. A private police report in leaked in 1989 identified Einem as the primary suspect in the case.

The Family Murders

From 1973 to 1983, a group of men is believed to have been involved in the abduction, rape, and murder of a series of young men and male teenagers in the Adelaide area. Five teens were killed during this time period, including Alan Barnes (aged 16), Neil Muir (aged 25), Peter Stogneff (aged 14), Mark Langley (aged 18), and Richard Kelvin (aged 15). All victims were abducted and subjected to extended bouts of torture and physical assault, including sexual assault and medical experimentation.

Bevan Spencer von Einem was convicted of the abduction and murder of Richard Kelvin 1984 and is currently serving life in prison in Port Augusta prison. In 1990, he was also charged with the murder of Alan Barnes and Mark Langley, but key evidence from the Richard Kelvin murder was ruled inadmissible in the trial. Following the ruling against this key evidence, the prosecution dropped these charges against Einem on December 21, 1990.

Although Einem was the only member of this group to be convicted, and four out of five of The Family Murders remain unsolved, law enforcement officials believe that Einem was part of a white-collar group that preyed on young children. He remains the prime, and only living, suspect in the disappearance of the Beaumont children.

Impact on the Parents

Jim and Nancy Beaumont continued to hold out hope of finding their children for several decades after their disappearance. In fact, the couple continued to live at the Somerton Park home, at 109 Harding Street, that they shared with their children for nearly two decades, hoping that the children would return home someday. Nancy Beaumont was reported as saying that it would be "dreadful" if the children returned to the home only to find that their parents had moved.

"The Beaumonts left the rooms of the children untouched," Orange said. "Every toy, every book even the bed was left exactly as the children had left them."

The couple were never considered as suspects in the case and cooperated with the police at every turn in the investigation, including working with the police and searching in vain every time a new lead developed in the case over the next several decades.

According to The Age, the parents "have since separated, but still live in Adelaide." The stress and sorrow that resulted from their children's abduction, combined with the constant new leads and media attention is said to have contributed to the failure of their marriage.

Jim, in particular, is said to still be suffering from intense and inconsolable grief every time a new development is reported. Nancy was also reported to have suffered extreme grief and horror when, in 1990, several Australian newspapers released computer-generated images of what her children would look like after aging several decades. She reportedly refused to look at the pictures.

"Jim was a little bit stronger than Nancy," Orange said. "He would address the media more than she did. But they both suffered terribly for the rest of their lives into their eighties. They would spend over fifty years wishing for their children's return, getting false hope after false hope, one false lead after another which would all ultimately turn up nothing. It was a horrific cruelty."

Lastly, Jim and Nancy have largely been seen as sympathetic and pitiable figures in the Australian media and in society at large. Although their actions may seem reckless or irresponsible by today's standards, Australian society was viewed as extremely safe in the 1960s and their policy of allowing a child to supervise their younger siblings both in the home and in public was practiced by a large portion of Australian parents.

Impact on Australian Society

The disappearance of the Beaumont children became an overnight sensation in Australia, led to one of the largest police searches in the country's history, and remains the most famous missing persons case in the country. Prior to this incident, Australia was largely viewed as one of the safest societies on the planet and children were allowed to roam freely, doors remained unlocked at all times, and there was little fear of strangers. All of that changed overnight.

"Australia lost its innocence with the disappearance of the Beaumont Children," Orange said. "For three young children to disappear was unheard of. The city where they grew up was a dignified place, a safe place. But it was all an illusion that went away the day the children went missing."

During the initial search for the children, Jim Beaumont went on national television to appeal for their safe return. His heartfelt address to the nation had a lasting impact on the parents and children who watched his plea. Hundreds of viewers called into the station to offer tips and Australian police report that hundreds of tips continue to come in every year to this day. His image on national television continues to serve as a warning for those who believe in the incorruptibility of their fellow citizens and in the safety of their country.

"A lot of people today will blame the parents for letting them go on the bus alone," Adelaide resident Rachel Harding said. "But times were different back then. Back then kids would walk to school by themselves. Kids were told not to talk to strangers. The Beaumonts did tell their children to not talk to children. But child molesters are cunning monsters. My guess is that he may have stolen the eldest child's purse then conned them into seeing him as their benefactor. They would not have had money to get home then along comes this "blonde man" who offers them money. Buys them food and promises to take them home."

Children who came of age in Australia during the 1960s have remarked that there was a definite culture shift following the Beaumont children's disappearance, often describing a "before" and "after." While children were once allowed to roam freely and interact with strangers, Australian parents have since altered their style of parenting and curtailed the amount of freedom offered to young children.

"It was the type of case where we believe there was a lone offender," Australian police detective Des Bray said. "It isn't the type of crime where one would go around bragging about. But we do hope that he told someone and that somebody knows something."

If the Beaumont children are alive today, they would all be in their 50s and would have lived through years of hearing their names and story broadcast on national television and reported on breathlessly in national newspapers. Despite the vast amount of information we have on the case, their fates may never be known with any certainty.

Both Jim and Nancy Beaumont are still alive, and as of this writing they are ninety and eighty-years old respectively. The anonymous tips and false hopes continue to come in today as they did over fifty years ago.

THE MISSING BEAUTY QUEEN : THE DISAPPEARANCE OF TARA GRINSTEAD

AMANDA DARLING

"I'm an 11th-grade history teacher at Irwin County High school. I also have a cheerleading squad of Junior Varsity cheerleaders. I just completed my first year of teaching, and I love every bit of it." - Tara Grinstead in a 1999 interview.

Tara Grinstead was a beauty pageant winner and high school teacher who strangely disappeared on October 22nd, 2005.

The mystery of her disappearance is as baffling now as it was over ten years ago. Tara was a beautiful woman in a small town and drew the attention of many men. But as investigators peeled back the onion on her life, they discovered that she had a complex personal life, one with many lovers and layers of relationship any one of whom may have sought to do her harm out of jealousy.

Investigators have pieced together the timeline of her activities prior to her disappearance. But the missing piece lies sometime during the night of October 22nd, 2005, when someone abducted Tara Grinstead and she would never be seen again.

What happened to Tara Grinstead?

EARLY LIFE

Tara was born on November 14th, 1974 to Faye and Billy Grinstead. She grew up in Hawkinsville, Georgia and was a popular cheerleader in high school as well as a diligent student. Her parents would divorce and her father would remarry a woman named Connie to whom Tara grew close to as well.

Tara loved animals, singing and going to church as a kid.

One cannot look upon pictures and video of Tara and not remark that she had a striking beauty. Graced with a voluptuous figure and long black hair, she had the ability to light up any room she walked into. She would eventually compete in beauty pageants, falling in love with the preparation, competition, and glamor of the activity.

"She had been into so many (pageants) that I had lost count," Connie Grinstead said.

Tara meticulously prepared for the pageants, remaining physically fit, taking speech lessons and learning how to sing. She would also graduate from Middle Georgia College and become a teacher at Irwin County High School in Ocilla. She would teach history to 11th graders but not give up on her pageant hopes.

In 1999, she would achieve the first step in her dream to enter the Miss USA contest, when she would win the local title of Miss Tifton.

This victory would allow her to compete in the Miss Georgia pageant. She would also receive scholarship winnings that she would use to help pay for her continuing college education.

"It was, for her, more than a dream come true," Tara's best friend Maria Hulett said. "It was the chance for her to be really proud of herself."

Footage of Tara during the Georgia pageant showed her to be an exuberant woman with a zest for life. She loved to exercise, drink Diet Coke with grenadine, collect Barbies and listening to 80s music like Bon Jovi. She had an infectious smile and played to the camera as she showed off her yellow business suit that she would wear for the pageant interview.

"Why did you pick yellow?" the reporter asked.

"Because it shows that I'm a happy person," Tara said.

With her pageant days behind her, Tara would earn a master's degree in education from Valdosta State University.

"She wanted to be a principal," her friend Oshja Anderson said. "She was well on her way."

Always seeking to improve herself, Tara would teach classes during the day and go to graduate school at night. She also held down a part-time job selling cosmetics at the local department store. By 2005, she had applied for a doctoral program in history and would occasionally fill in as the assistant principal.

"On the surface," forensic psychiatrist Orange said. "Tara's life looked to be a stellar one. She had a bright future in academia and during her pageant days, she learned to put forward the best appearance. But what lurked underneath in her personal life is the mystery."

MARCUS HARPER

At the heart of Tara's disappearance is figuring out the type of relationships she had with the numerous men in her life. She worked as a teacher, went to night school and worked the cosmetics counter at a department store. Outgoing and bubbly, she didn't have the personality type to reject anyone out of hand. She attracted men and had many suitors.

She did have a longtime boyfriend in Marcus Harper.

Harper was an Ocilla police officer who would later become an Army Ranger. Both of Tara's parents liked him as they both expressed the fact that he always remained respectful of them. They have consistently maintained that they never witnessed Harper treating Tara with disrespect.

Tara, however, had expressed to her sister that she was afraid of Marcus.

"She said she was afraid of him," Tara's sister Anita said. "What he had gone through with the Ranger training. He was capable of anything."

"Marcus was a strong Alpha-male type," Orange said. "A cop and an Army Ranger. Tara was rumored to have dated another cop as well but she didn't appear to have a type. From what we can gather, she dated a slew of men from older to younger, and from different walks of life."

About a year prior to her disappearance, Tara had broken up with Marcus. She had given him an ultimatum and wanted to be married. He did not want marriage but wanted to remain committed. The relationship would turn sour at that point.

Tara would begin to date other people. She was in a car with a romantic suitor named Rhett Roberts who was the son of her landlord.

Marcus spotted the couple and would go ballistic, shouting obscenities at Tara.

Despite this angry confrontation, Tara would maintain ties with Marcus. In late July or early August of 2005 they would go to St. Augustine on a beach trip. After their date, Tara would confide to a friend that she was concerned about Marcus's temper.

Marcus would then be deployed back to Iraq a few weeks later. Tara would write the Army Ranger a letter in which she effectively ended their relationship.

According to Marcus, however, their relationship didn't come to a close until October of 2005. He had returned from the Middle East and called Tara to tell her that their relationship was over. Tara was at work and became so distraught that had to pull over to the side of the road. She called a friend who came and took her home. The next day, Tara would call off sick from her teaching job in order to "take a mental health day."

There was a rumor that a cop from a neighboring town, Heath Dykes, came to visit Tara at her school shortly afterward.

"These behaviors certainly show some mental fragilities on the parts of both Tara and Marcus," Orange said. "From what we can gather, it looked like an off-and-on style relationship with a few other romantic partners thrown in for good measure. It is unclear as to who was chasing who at various points of their relationship. If we are to believe Marcus, then she was chasing him. If we are to believe Tara's sister, then she was afraid of him. Why would you chase a man that you were afraid of? Something is not right here."

A few days later, Tara and Marcus would have another "heated argument" which she would tell one of her friends at her night class as well as another friend the next day while she had lunch.

According to Marcus, the argument centered around him breaking up with her. But Tara's sister Anita Gattis had a different story.

"They had a very bad argument," Anita said. "Several days before she went missing, concerning an 18-year-old that he was dating. My sister did not think that (the 18-year-old's) parents would approve of a 30-year-old dating an-18-year-old. I'm told that she threatened to tell the parents and they had a very heated argument over this."

Marcus said the argument was about something else entirely. He stated that she begged him not to end their relationship.

"She wanted me back and all," Marcus said. "And I said, 'I've started shopping outside of Ocilla, I think you need to do the same. Everybody in this town is connected to us one way or another."

"She approached me crying," Harper said as he repeated the same story on Greta Van Susteren's TV show. "She was very irrational, and she told me that if she found out I was dating someone, she would commit suicide."

But Tara's friend Osjha disputes the fact that Tara would do or say something like that.

"She's never said anything remotely similar to me ever any time."

Law enforcement authorities don't believe Tara committed suicide as she would have to go to extreme lengths to hide her own body and would have no motive to do so.

"There are a couple of contradictory things at play here," Orange said. "Tara was rumored to have dated some of her students so it would be hypocritical of her to criticize Marcus for dating someone in their teens. And it also doesn't make sense for her to come to Marcus' home begging to get back together. She had her share of suitors, some coming from out of town. She was a beautiful woman and she had options."

To her family's dismay, both the authorities and press would place Tara's life under a microscope. They had discovered that she had "several romantic relationships that occurred in relative proximity to one another."

"There was more rumors and innuendo," Orange said. "There were rumors that she was dating Rhett Roberts, her landlord's son. Rumors that she was dating one of her teenage students. Rumors that she was dating Heath Dyke, a police officer from another county. Even her own brother-in-law, Larry Gattis, was rumored to have an affair with Tara."

Both Larry and Tara's sisters are physicians. Larry specializes in geriatric medicine with only 3.3 out of 5-star reviews on Healthgrades. He was interrogated by investigators and expressed his outrage at the questions they were asking. One question was that if he had an affair with Tara and his response was judged by the polygraph as "deceptive."

ALL THAT AND A STALKER TOO...

Tara would have a stalker in a former student named Anthony Vickers. Friends recalled that Tara had taken special care to tutor Vickers but she later realized that the young man was "unstable."

"He was just kind of a troubled kid and that would be her nature," Osjha said.

Vickers was obsessed with his beauty queen teacher and claimed to have had a romantic relationship with her.

"She talked about the fact that he would call and he would rely on her and she knew it was getting too much for her," a friend named Maria said. "I just kept telling her, 'You know Tara, something's wrong."

Vickers was two years out of high school when he came to Tara's house and demanded to be let in. He pounded on the door until she called the police. Vickers resisted arrest but charges were later dropped and no restraining orders were ever filed.

The Vickers incident wasn't the only occasion that the former beauty pageant winner was being stalked. There was an incident where someone would call her home and make threats. The call was traced and it was determined to be a student in her homeroom who was promptly removed from the class.

THE NIGHT OF...

Before the night of her disappearance, Tara had enjoyed the company of her friend Dana and some teenage girls as they readied for the "Miss Georgia Sweet Potato" pageant. Her friend remembered

Tara as being in a great mood, helping out the girls with their hair and makeup. She would attend the pageant where she served as a backstage coach. Later that evening, she went to the house of a neighbor before going to a barbecue a few blocks from her home . Police believe that she had remained at the barbecue until 11 pm when she left to go home. They would find the clothes she wore at the cookout on her bedroom floor which indicated to police that she had, in fact, returned home.

From that point on, police "have no idea" what happened to Tara.

On October 24th, 2005, Tara did not show up to teach her class. Her colleagues called the police who showed up at her residence to do a welfare check. They would find her white Mitsubishi parked in the garage, unlocked. Upon entering her home, police found a business card lodged in her door.

There appeared to be no sign of forced entry. Searching through the house, police found her cell phone plugged into her charger. Her purse and keys could not be found.

Strangely, the clothes she wore the night before were piled on the bedroom floor.

Investigators found it odd that the car door was unlocked and that the car seat was pushed back. Tara was petite at only five-foot-three and would have kept the seat much closer to the steering wheel. They found an envelope of cash (one hundred dollars) on her dashboard while both her dog and cat were inside. Tara's sister said that she was an animal lover who would never just abandon her pets.

Something was wrong...

The police immediately called the Georgia Bureau of Investigation as the lacked the resources to pursue this kind of crime.

Taking over the case, the GBI believed that Tara may have left with someone that she knew, given the lack of a forced entry and the fact that only her purse and keys were missing. Neighbors did not report hearing any screaming at night.

Her disappearance shocked the small and close-knit community. To a person, Tara was described as someone who had a great personality, loved by faculty and students alike. Nothing in her professional life would suggest that she had any enemies.

Volunteers from the community immediately went to work. Irwin County students, teachers, and other townsfolk searched the area and put out flyers.

"Missing. Tara Grinstead. $20,000 Reward."

ROUNDING UP THE SUSPECTS

Longtime boyfriend Marcus Harper was one of the first to be questioned. He came with a ready-made alibi for the night of Tara's disappearance.

Marcus was seen at a bar with friends then went on a 'ride-along' with a former partner on the local police force. His whereabouts was "essentially substantiated" according to authorities.

Former student/stalker Anthony Vickers was questioned but later ruled out as a suspect. Like the others, however, he could not account for the entire thirty-four hour period when Tara was last seen and reported missing.

"Vickers is probably the only one I would rule out," Orange said. "This disappearance was too clean. Vickers was a disturbed twenty-year-old man with a crush. He would not have the emotional wherewithal or the knowledge to pull off a crime with no clues. But someone with law enforcement or medical training could."

But who left the business card behind at her door?

The card was left by Heath Dykes, a married Perry police officer with two children. He was from the next town over and had known Tara since high school.

Neighbors would tell investigators that he visited Tara's house often. It is unclear what their relationship was (outside of the obvious innuendo and rumors).

Still, he had left close to two dozen messages on Tara's answering message on the weekend she went missing.

There is small-town gossip that the two were having an affair. Local witnesses have confirmed that they saw his wife throw his clothes out on the front lawn. The content of the messages he left have not been made public but the rumors were that he was telling her "he was sorry" and that he "loved her."

What is clear is that he did call Tara's mother from the front yard and ask if she knew where Tara was and if she was alright.

Heath Dykes was the last known person at Tara's home that night as he arrived a little after midnight.

"There are simply too many secrets here," Orange said. "Something was clearly going on in Heath's mind in order for him to call Tara that many times over the course of one evening. One rumor is that they were having an affair and that she was going to tell his wife. So he was calling her in a desperate attempt to stop her from doing that. Another possibility was that she was calling him for help and he was returning her calls. His involvement led to a lot of outlandish speculation, one of which was that Heath knew that a hit man was coming for Tara and that he was calling to make sure that she was okay."

"I think the fact that she was beautiful and other people paid attention to her would obviously make some people jealous," Tara's friend Maria said. "I think she was afraid of the possibility of someone hurting her from being angry at her, having reactions to her dating people."

Numerous men were rounded up and questioned, there was Jim Perry who dated Tara years earlier, Rhett Roberts, Marcus Harper, Anthony Vickers, and Eric Cook among others.

Another unsubstantiated rumor that Tara was involved with another student named Eric Cook. A friend of his had made mention of their affair in an Internet forum post where he stated that everyone knew that they were "messing around." He also said that the police didn't make the information public out of respect for Tara's family as she dated around quite a bit. An alleged friend of Cook disputed the rumor on the forum, however. Cook would later die in a car accident.

A neighbor, Joe Poirier lived with his wife and was rumored to have been "obsessed" with Tara. The older couple admitted to "looking out for Tara" and they were fond of her. He was seen pouring concrete near his home the day after she disappeared.

Another person of interest was Larry Gattis, the brother-in-law of Tara. He was brought in for questioning after the disappearance. It would later be revealed that he had been asked if he had an affair with Tara.

Larry answered 'no'.

The polygraph machine marked it as a 'deceptive answer.'

48 HOURS

In 2008, Tara's case would be featured on the CBS News show "48 Hours Mystery." The show would illustrate the parallels between Tara's case and the disappearance of Jennifer Kesse who would go missing in Orlando, Florida three months later. The GBI would also reveal during the broadcast that they had found a latex glove in Tara's yard just a few feet away from her front porch.

The GBI forensic team would analyze the DNA left in the glove and determine that it was a man's DNA, they just do not know who it belongs to. They would compare the DNA samples of the numerous men who were associated with or knew Tara but none of them have matched.

The DNA has also been entered into the Georgia and national databases but no match has been made to date.

"The glove may be a red herring," Orange said. "Whoever entered the home left nothing behind, no prints, DNA, nothing. So it was obviously someone who knew exactly what they were doing. They wanted to harm Tara."

A HOAX AND FALSE TIPS

In February of 2009, a man calling himself the "Catch Me Killer" began posting videos boasting that he had murdered sixteen women. One of the women he described had a close resemblance to Tara Grinstead. The man producing the video digitally obscured his face and voice but police eventually identified the culprit as twenty-seven-year-old Andrew Haley.

Haley performed the videos as part of a bizarre hoax and was eliminated as a possible suspect.

Investigator Gary Rothwell has expressed his lament at how the rumors and speculation have caused unfair stress to many who have been already tried in the public eye. "Irresponsible public accusations have been made about them, and they have no way to respond or defend themselves. And it's frustrating that we don't have evidence to rule anyone in or out."

Rothwell admits, however, that he has information that has not been released.

In February of 2015, authorities acted on a tip which led them to drain a pond in Fitzgerald, Georgia.

They didn't go into details as to what the specifics of the tip were. The pond would be drained and nothing would be found.

ALIBIS

Police have alibis from all the men who knew Tara Grinstead but no one has been ruled out because no one can account for the full thirty-four hour period.

Rhett Reynolds stated he went to sleep after the cookout. Joe Poirier was with his wife next door.

The most elaborate alibi, however, came from Marcus Harper.

Again, Marcus was in a local bar and a friend of Tara's had spotted him there. She would call Tara at around 10:15 and 10:30 to tell Tara that Marcus was there.

After 1 am, Marcus left the bar and went to look for his police officer friend, Sgt. Sean Fletcher. Fletcher was on duty that night.

Fletcher knew Tara as well. Ironically, he was one of the officers who arrived at Tara's house when Anthony Vickers, Tara's former student, was banging on her door.

There were rumors that Tara didn't like Fletcher because he had told Harper that Tara was entertaining Heath Dykes at her home.

Fletcher would deny that speculation.

"What we can extrapolate from this scenario was that Vickers was angry that his crush, Tara, was with another man," Orange said. "So he goes to her home and demands that she talk to him. He's young, twenty-years-old, and doesn't understand why she would do this to him. He is then arrested by Fletcher who relays what Tara is doing to Marcus, a man that Tara is wary about because of his temper. So now we have more than just a love triangle, it is a love octagon, with numerous men vying for and getting jealous over the attention of Tara."

At around 1:49 am, Fletcher received a call from dispatch informing him that Marcus Harper was looking for him. The two met up and walked Fletcher's beat, checking doors in downtown Ocilla.

Around 2:45, Fletcher was dispatch to a home where a mentally unbalanced man, Bennie Merritt, had stumbled into a home and refused to leave. Marcus would join Fletcher on the call as did two other officers. Merritt, however, was gone from the premises.

Minutes later, they began to search for Merritt who was also a neighbor of Tara's. The drunken Merritt would accost the cashier at the local gas station then be apprehended. Both Fletcher and Harper had responded to the call at the gas station and by the time they were done it was 4:28 am.

Marcus then headed home.

Investigators would later be able to corroborate these details with multiple witnesses, including Merritt, who was scrutinized as a possible suspect in the kidnapping as well.

Marcus Harper, however, has not been ruled out as a potential person of interest in the case.

"Marcus's alibi is too perfect," GBI investigator Maurice Godwin said.

Both Larry and Anita Gattis believe that Marcus is the top suspect.

"He had the motive," Tara's sister said. "And the training."

The insinuation would draw the ire of Marcus who became upset that Anita consistently brought up his military and police training. He continues to deny any involvement in Tara's disappearance.

"I don't wanna hurt any innocent civilian much less someone I spent five and a half years of my life with."

"What is clear is that there isn't a whole lot forthcoming about Tara's personal life to draw the conclusions we need to about who is the most probable suspect," Orange said. "Like in the Natalee Holloway case, the sexual activity of the woman in question is kept hidden. If her background reveals that she was a promiscuous woman, there will e less sympathy and urgency to solve the crime. That is one of the more striking aspects of the case, aside from Tara's vanishing, is the cover-up of Tara's personal life in order to protect her reputation."

UNSOLVABLE CASE?

Tara Grinstead's case is still being investigated. The GBI reports that they receive numerous leads per day, most of which are false.

Her body has never been found but her impact on the lives of those around her and her students will never be forgotten.

"I'm so sorry to hear about what happened to Miss Grinstead," said Christine Kang, a South Korean exchange student from Grinstead's class. "She is so caring and giving to her students. I am sure she will come home soon safely. I will pray for her every night."

KILLER MISTRESS: THE TRUE STORY OF TANIA HERMAN

58

LINDA CARLISLE

Tania Lee-Anne Herman, better known in the Australian media as the body-in-the-boot or Mum-in-the-boot killer, was born in Rochester in 1996, just south of the city of Echuca. Echuca is a small town located on the banks of the Murray River and the Campaspe River in Victoria, with its name meaning "Meeting of the Waters" in the local Aboriginal dialect. The town has a population of just over 13 000 and is known as the paddle steamer capital of Australia. Tania was born into a simple, country family. She was the youngest of four children, and she enjoyed a safe and inspiring childhood. Tania was a promising junior swimmer, having won several titles at the state level, and had an incredible flair for the arts. Her lawyer, Julie Sutherland, commented later in her life that Tania "was the embodiment and quintessence of everything noble and decent which one comes to equate with country living, including a strong work ethic and getting on with life despite its vicissitudes." As a high school student, she made money on the side by creating floral bridal hairpieces. None of her friends or family members would have said that Tania was suffering from any difficulties in her younger life, from an early age Tania learned to hide things that were causing her grief. This became something that was characteristic of her throughout her life in an attempt to not cause concern for others.

Before she met "soul mate" Joe Korp who would eventually manipulate Tania into actions that would deprive her of twelve years of freedom, Tania had three significant relationships that left her in a damaged and compromised position. She also endured years of sexual abuse as a child, which she was told was "a special kind of love". When she was older, Tania's first marriage was to John Linton on Sep 26th, 1987 when she was just seventeen. Linton was older than Tania, and their relationship only lasted five months. After this time, Tania met a Columbian student when she was twenty-one and they had a two-year romance. During this time, Tania had her first child, but her partner was cheating on her and Herman eventually found out about the other woman. Her boyfriend left, and later married the woman that he was cheating on Tania with. Finally, in 1996, Tania married Paul Herman who was a charter boat operator in Queensland. Things seemed that they might start to become more stable for Herman. They had Tania's second daughter and moved back to Echuca. However, her husband was a big drinker. Tania reported that her husband would at least go through several slabs and a bottle of bourbon each week and that this began to concern her. However, the real issue for Tania was when Paul became physically violent towards the end of their relationship. In Tania's opinion, this behavior was fueled by his dependency on alcohol and she didn't see a future for them if this continued. Tania left Paul in 2002.

When Tania was 30, she was diagnosed with cervical cancer and had to undergo chemotherapy and radiation therapy for six months. Tania decided not to tell her family about her health issues. When she lost her hair, she claimed that she had shaved it for charity. Tania's desire to keep the troubling news to herself might have made it easier for the manipulative man who was about to arrive on the scene and ask more of Tania than she ever believed she would be capable of doing. After a string of unsuccessful relationships and marriages, Tania, a vulnerable single mother of two, went in search of a new partner online. Unfortunately for her, she stumbled across Joe Korp.

Joe Korp, who was registered on the dating site as Joe Bonte, was posing as a single, self-employed builder. The factory worker was married to Maria Korp, a woman who had immigrated to Australia from Portugal with an earlier, failed marriage. Maria helped to build their house in North Melbourne, being the project bricklayer on the house and directly involved in much of its construction. Unfortunately, almost immediately after they moved in both partners began to express unhappiness in their marriage. Maria had a daughter, Laura, from a previous marriage, and she and Joe had their son Damien together early on in their marriage. When Joe initially connected with Tania in a chat room in October of 2003, he kept his marriage to Maria a secret. There are conflicting claims from different prosecutors as to when Tania became aware of the marriage, some claiming early on and others maintaining that Tania wasn't aware for up to 12 months into their relationship. Whether Tania found out about Maria earlier or later is not of great concern, as this information did nothing to deter her from meeting up with Joe and planning their future life together. During this time, Joe was also seeking out other relationships online, but he provided Tania with a sense of security that he had been searching for her for his whole life. Sources did not report whether or not be actually met up with other women, but the frequency with which he was away from home and the number of times that he was visiting Tania suggest that he had several women. This period may have even been a test for several of these women as to who Joe determined would be capable of killing in the name of their love for him.

The first time that Joe drove to Echuca to meet Tania in February 2004, she showed him the sights around town before having sex in his car down by the Murray River. Joe made many trips like this one over the coming months, hiring cars for the drive and telling Maria that he was in Sydney on business. Joe began to promise Tania the world, even going as far to say that he wanted to buy wedding rings together and have a ceremony in her house as a sort of temporary marriage until they were able to have a real one. Joe promised children to Tania, a long life together, and her much-craved stability. From the moment that she met Joe, Tania began to act as if she was under a spell. Even Tania's lease was registered under the name of Tania Herman Korp. When Paul Herman, one of Tania's previous husbands, had a heart attack while working on a paddleboat, Joe attended the funeral with her. Paul's family later remembered his face when Maria's case was all over the television and newspapers, and some have even wondered whether Pau's death might have occurred under suspicious circumstances. When Joe spoke to Tania, he described his then present marriage as unhappy and sexless, telling Tania how much he was looking forward to the life that they could share together when he was no longer with Maria. Joe assured Tania that the only reason that he hadn't already left Maria was that Maria held incriminating evidence against him and had threatened to take this information to the police if he ever left her. Joe never specified what this information was, holding a lot of things back from Tania. Herman, however, couldn't see this approach.

At this time, Joe became manipulative and domineering. Joe told Tania that he preferred her to only wear black, so those were the clothes that she donned. He told her to distance herself from her friends, so she became isolated. In a prison interview after the death of Maria Korp, Tania divulged information about her mindset at the time. "I think I was sort of brainwashed by him because I was so in love with him and he used to promise me the world — that we'd be married and we'd have a house and we'd have a family and ... it's just one thing after another," she claimed. Eventually, Joe even went so far as to ask her to move closer to him. Tania sold her house and moved to Greendale, by this time acutely aware of Maria and Joe's children. All this time, Joe was finding and meeting up with other women online just as he had done with Tania, but she was unaware of this fact. It is also likely that Joe began to see more of Tania at this time due to her closer location, and that this led to Maria confirming her suspicions that her husband had a mistress. Little did Maria know that events were falling into place that would eventually result in her assault, attempted murder, and death.

In Greendale, Tania enrolled her youngest daughter at the same school as Joe and Maira's son Damien. She even went so far as to list Joe as the emergency contact for her child at the school's office. By this time, Maria was aware that Joe was having an affair. One day, Joe came home to the locks changed and all of his belongings on the lawn. Maria had told friends and relatives about the weekends she spent alone as Joe was on his 'business trips'. During this time, Joe moved in with Tania and he met members of her family, including her brother Stephen Deegan. However, after a brief period, Joe returned to Maria on Christmas Eve. He phoned Tania to assure her that there was still hope for them together, and this is when the pair first began to plot the death of Maria Korp. Tania has stated that the plans began up to a year before the day that she waited for Maria in her garage. During this year, there were a variety of plans including staging a burglary where Joe could bash her to death, and running over Maria with a car. Joe even looked into the cost of hiring a hit man. However, in the end, they settled on Tania taking Maria's life, or what Joe always referred to as "taking care" of his wife, or "getting her out of the road." As the two continued to discuss these ideas, they moved away from a fantasy where they might be able to live together and closer towards practical actions. It is difficult to say whether Joe genuinely wanted to live with Tania and have a future with her. Perhaps if there had been less of an investigation into the matter and he didn't feel the need to incriminate Tania there would have been room for such a life. Either way, at this point, Tanis had no doubts that everything that they were planning was for the future of their love.

During Joe Korps's stay at Tania's house, they discussed how to kill Maria at a pre-Christmas barbecue where her brother Stephen was present. Stephen later contacted the police on the 14th of February regarding the disappearance of Maria Korp, stating that his sister and Joe had talked about several ways of killing Maria in front of Stephen, including using a belt as a ligature. They also asked for Stephen's opinion, saying "What's the best way to knock someone off?" Stephen said that he had encouraged his sister to break off all contact with Joe, and that he "Was crazy and that she should get rid of this guy". As he told police about her reluctance to stop seeing Joe, he noted that it was "Like he had brainwashed her." Stephen also mentioned that in late January Joe was present again and that he and Tania spoke freely in front of Stephen about killing Maria. Furthermore, the night before Maria's disappearance, Tania called Stephen and asked that he visit her as she had something to discuss. During this phone call, Tanis was considerably distressed and going through a moral dilemma. The following is Stephen's account of that discussion as he stated it to the police:

"Tania told me that she and Jo were going to kill Maria. She was very matter of fact about it, and it was like she had already done it. She told me that she was going to use thin cotton gloves, dye her hair, use a swimming cap and black beanie over the top. She also told me what clothes she was going to wear. She said that Jo was going to pick her up and take her to his place. On the way, they would stop and she would get into the boot so that he could smuggle her in. Then she was going to hide behind his car and wait for Maria. She would then sneak up behind her and try to strangle her with a belt. After this, she would put her in the boot of the car and drive the car to the Shrine in Melbourne."

On the morning of the 9th February 2005, Joe Korp drove Tania to his Mount Ridley address at around 6:00AM where she was to lay wait in the garage until Maria came down to drive to work. Joe and Tania had a short conversation in the garage, where he assured her that he loved her. Tania later recounted to police that Joe asked her "How much do you love me? Are you going to show me today?" and also told her that she must make sure that Maria doesn't leave the garage alive. "You've got to get rid of her for me. I want her strangled. I want her dead." Tania had dyed her hair and was wearing the swimming cap, gloves, and black beanie, just as she had told Stephen she would. She hid behind Laura's car and began to rationalize what she was about to do. As she sat there with the strap, and remembers thinking "I shouldn't be doing this. It's not right." Joe had already left for work and the only thing that allowed her to continue the act was repeating Joe's words over and over in her head again that she mustn't let Maria out of the garage alive. In this way, she became somewhat distanced from her actions and it allowed her to go through with the tasks that lay ahead.

When Maria came down the stairs, Tania hooked the strap over Maria's neck and began to apply pressure. Maria screamed and they both tumbled to the ground, Maria fighting for her life and Tania fighting for love. Tania, being physically stronger and larger than Maria, was able to overpower her and won the struggle through sheer force. During these moments, Tania continued to ethically struggle with the actions that saw she herself committing, later saying that "I was in a set frame of mind, but as soon as I saw the blood, something snapped. I panicked," she says. But yet again, by keeping Joe's words in her mind she was able to get through the ordeal. Eventually, Maria slumped down onto the ground and stopped moving. Tania picked her up and dumped Maria in the boot of her own car before taking the keys and preparing to drive to the Shrine of Remembrance in Melbourne. "As I was driving, I couldn't stop crying. I kept thinking, 'This is wrong, this is wrong," Tania claims. On the way, Tania would hear Maria breathing in the boot and came to the realization that she wasn't dead. She heard other sounds as she drove, but didn't know what she could do about the situation. When she got out of the car, the considered other actions that she might take, but settled on leaving Maria in the boot to die. This added another layer to Tania's ethical dilemma, as the death had not been clean cut. For days she would be forced to think about the fact that the woman was still alive in the car, and that every moment that she wasn't going back to retrieve her she was condemning her to death. The only thing that brought her any clarity at this time was the knowledge that now the hardest part was done, and that if they were able to get through the police investigation she and Joe would be able to start the new life that they had spoken so much about. However, Tania was soon to find out that Joe would betray her in his interviews where he would name her as the likely killer.

After parking Maria's car at the Shrine of Remembrance, Tania rushed to Stephen's work on Elizabeth Street in Melbourne at 8:30AM. She asked her brother to drive her to her home in Greenville and seemed calm and collected. Tania told Stephen that she had done as she claimed she would, and killed Maria Korp. Stephen had not previously contacted the police as he didn't believe that his sister would be truly capable of these crimes. Even when she arrived at his workplace and openly confessed, he still didn't believe she had truly done it and took this as one more step to mislead him. Stephen was extremely worried for his sister, and would make fresh attempts to encourage her not to be in contact with Joe, but he was certain that the events that Tania was claiming had passed were either figments of her imagination or attempts at some guise. It wasn't until he saw the news coverage when Maria was found in the boot four days later that he accepted his sister's crimes and called the police to fill in as many details as he could. Tania then met up with Joe and gave over the keys to Maria's car. She told Joe that she was concerned that she hadn't successfully killed Maria, and so that he was "taking a life." Joe allegedly replied: "No, you took the life for me," and soothed Tania, maintaining that she would not be caught. Joe told her to go out into the Lake Eppalock area and burn all of the items that implicated them in the crime. These items included not only the gloves, beanie, swimming cap, and belt that Tania had used at the scene, but also a number of other things that the couple has used as they planned the assault. Other items were also later buried at the Greenvale Reservoir. Later that evening, Joe Korp reported Maria as missing

to the Craigieburn Police.

When Joe was interviewed the next morning, the police discussed his relationship with his wife, their financial position, their working commitments, and Joe's connection with Tania Herman. During this interview, Joe was asked if he could think of anybody that would want to hurt Maria, and he immediately told the police that he believed Tania had done it. Joe claimed that Tania wished ill will of Maria and that she was jealous of their marriage. He denied any involvement in the disappearance of his wife, and Joe also claimed that he was slowing down the relationship with Tania. The police then interviewed Herman, who was described as being very cooperative with the police but maintained not only that she hadn't been involved with the crime, but that she had never met Maria and didn't know her. When Tania was released on this day, she attempted to make contact with Joe. She tried to connect with him twenty times through calls and messages, but he didn't respond to any of them. It was around this time that Tania started to wonder whether Joe was planning this all along, and had used her to get out of his marriage with Maria safely and without allegations regarding the sensitive material that his wife had claimed she held. She now began to feel that she had been thrown under the bus, doing Joe's dirty work for him and bound to get stuck with the consequences.

The search for Maria Korp continued for four long days until a gardener recognized her car from the news bulletins. Those who opened the boot claim that they thought Maria was already dead due to the stench and the state of her body. When they realized that she was breathing, Maria was rushed to the Alfred Hospital and put into intensive care. The initial diagnosis was that she had suffered from strangulation, dehydration, and prolonged loss of consciousness, which had resulted in brain injury. Later on that day, Maria was examined by Forensic Physician Dr. Morris Odell, who categorized which injuries were a result of the initial struggle and which were a result of her incarceration in the boot of the car. Odell noted that her neck injuries were likely caused by the application of a ligature. Maria stayed in a coma, and she

was fed intravenously before being moved onto nasogastric feeding before percutaneous entrogastric tube feeding. The doctors monitored her neurological state with MRIs, which showed a progressive loss of brain substance which suggested that her initial diagnosis of having a severe hypoxic brain injury was accurate. When Maria did not improve over months, the decision was made on the 27th July to cease her medical management and tube feeding as her condition was perceived to be terminal. At fifty years old, Maria Korp died in Alfred Hospital at 2:40AM on the 5th August 2005.

On the afternoon of the 16th February 2005, both Joe and Tania were interviewed once more. For the third time, Joe was interviewed and maintained his stance that he had nothing to do with the attempted murder of his wife. Joe made no comment on the questions that were asked of him, and Tania Herman made full admissions to not only her involvement in the attempted murder but details about Joe being her accomplice. By this time, Tania had realized Joe's intentions to pin the entire event on her and had begun to wake up from her spellbound period of infatuation with him. Even though she still loved Joe dearly, she felt that the truth about the situation had to be told. Tanis was charged with attempted murder. On the 1st July 2005, Tania was charged with twelve years imprisonment with a non-parole time of nine years. Joe Korp, who was charged and remanded in custody, had been released on the 9th June to stand before the Supreme Court on the 3rd August. Joe wrote a letter to Tania, which he had his sister deliver. In this, he insisted that there was still a chance for them if she wanted it. "I think I was sort of brainwashed by him because I was so in love with him and he used to promise me the world — that we'd be married and we'd have a house and we'd have a family and ... it's just one thing after another," Tania claimed. Over the years to come, through the counseling that she would receive in the prison system and the friends that she would make there, Tania would come to understand that way that Joe treated her. These new perspectives would give her a whole new outlook on these years of her life and the ways in which he was treating her.

On the day of Maria's funeral, Joe went out into the shed of the house that he shared with Maria. He wrote a series of diary entries, notes, and letters, and stuck up pictures of Maria on the shed walls. Joe hung himself, and one of the notes which were left close to where he was found hanging read "F-ck all those who thought I was guilty" and "Where's the justice...no f———evidence." In all of these letters and diary entries, he maintained his innocence and his love for Maria. In one letter to a daughter of his, Mia, from a previous marriage, he wrote:

"Mia, Oh my only daughter.

"I have loved you and cried for you all my life.

"It was nice to see you and become close again.

"Please forgive me for leaving you again.

"Please understand about love.

"I found it and lost it with Maria.

"Stupid me."

At this time, Herman was devastated. In one session with the prison counselor, she revealed: "If he's not alive I don't want to live." Tania went into a long period of silence after this, resistant to talking about the case with anybody who came by to interview her. Eventually, she opened up to one writer, Rochelle Jackson, who was putting together a collection called Partners in Crime: The true stories of eight women and their lives with notorious men which were published in 2012 by Allen and Unwin. It is from these interviews that we have come to understand so much more about Tania and the experiences that she went through. It is also due to this text that we can gain some insight into how she was reflecting on her actions and her time with Joe. During this interview, Tania expressed to the world that her biggest regret was taking a mother away from her children, eleven-year-old Damien and twenty-seven year old Laura. Tania, a mother herself, found herself haunted by this fact and named this as the place where she harbored the most guilt regarding the whole series of events. Tania only had sporadic contact with her own daughters during her jail sentence. Eventually, Tania began to show signs of accepting the things that she had done and wanting to grow past them: "I've done his crime and now I'm doing his time. The past is the past and I can't undo it — I just have to move on."

Tania was initially incarcerated in the Dame Phyllis Frost maximum security prison. It is Victoria's largest women's prison, holding 260 prisoners, and dedicated to the philanthropist Dame Phyllis Frost, who was particularly concerned with the welfare of female prisoners. Aside from Prison Tarrengower which is a minimum security prison, which Tania was later transferred to, The Dame Phyllis Frost Centre is the only women's prison in Victoria. Aside from Tania Herman, there are several other prisoners who have spent time at the center that have captured Australian headlines. Vicky Roach, an indigenous activist, fought the High Court while in jail in a case that overturned an attempt to remove the vote from serving prisoners. Andrea Mohr, a German writer, served time for international drug smuggling and organized crime. Wendy Peirce, Roberta Williams, and Renate Mokbel were also inmates of the facility, both being figures in the Melbourne underworld as represented in the popular Underbelly series. However, probably the most famous inmate is Judy Moran who was the queen of the Melbourne underworld, murdering her brother-in-law Des "Tuppence" Moran. There are rumors that Herman and Moran had an altercation one day in the prison, but these allegations were denied by prison staff. The claim was that Herman had won a turf-war in the prison, with Moran having previously been the top dog. In the center, Herman was known as Muscles. Some sources claim that Tania punched Moran, and others claim that this turf-war was won purely on words. Tania was eventually moved from the maximum security prison to Tarrengower, where she began to pick up the pieces of her life.

Tarrengower held a lot of opportunities for Tania. During this time she began a degree in fine arts, took an interest in cooking, dressed up as Santa for the Christmas celebrations, and developed a friendship with her cellmate Bernadette Denny. Denny was in the system for the Herman Rockefeller murder which had occurred in January of 2010. Denny, an alcoholic pensioner, and her partner Mario Schembri, a sheet metal worker, got into contact with millionaire Rockefeller through an advertisement for couple swinging in a local newspaper. Herman claimed that he and his wife were interested in swinging together, but when he arrived he was alone, his wife knew nothing of the matter. Herman engaged in intercourse with Denny while Schembri watched, and promised to bring his wife the next time that he arrived. When he arrived frazzled one evening demanding sex of Denny with no wife in sight, the couple became aggressive. Rockefeller kept attempting to grab and sexually assault Denny, So Schembri and Rockefeller became involved in a brawl which Denny joined. This interaction became more and more violent until Rockefeller apparently fell over and knocked his dead, causing his death. After this, the couple went shopping for materials to dispose of the body, being seen on a hardware store camera buying plastic drop sheets and testing the weight of a chainsaw. They dismembered his body and Schembri took the remains to a friend's house where he burnt the parts over time. Tania became very close to Denny, and publically defended her as a good woman. During this time, Tania also met her current lover Nicky Muscat.

Nicky Muscat was in Tarrengower as a fraudster, having stolen $118 000 from the pokies venue that he had managed. During their time at Tarrengower, a relationship developed between Nicky and Tania and they even asked for a ceremony where they could be married behind bars. This event became highly publicized in the Australian media and brought a lot of attention back to the case. This request was denied, but their love stayed strong. On the 14th February 2014, Tania Herman was released from prison. Nicky, who had been released from the prison the year earlier, arrived to pick her up in a silver 4WD and took her to her home in Yarraville. Over the next few days, the couple was spotted walking around their local streets and stores hand-in-hand, with Tania beginning to pick up the pieces. Tania and Nicky are still together, adjusting to life on the outside and trying to make up for the time that they each lost in prison. Perhaps they offer each other an understanding that many people would not be capable of. Finally, Tania has found a relationship with the stability, respect, and understanding that she has always been looking for.

KILLER GRANNIES : TRUE STORIES OF SERIAL KILLING SENIORS

ERICA BYRAM

Dorothea Puente became infamous in the 1980s for being the "Death House Landlady". She ran a boarding home in Sacramento, California and proceeded to steal the Social Security checks of her elderly and mentally disabled tenants. Those tenants who proved to be too troublesome would be given increased dosages of sleeping pills until they died. She would chop up the bodies and bury them in her backyard.

EARLY LIFE

Dorothea Puente was born Dorothea Gray on January 9th, 1929 in Redlands, California. Both her mother, Trudy Mae, and her father Jesse James Gray, worked as cotton pickers in Central California. Her father would die of tuberculosis in 1937 while her mother would die the following year in a car accident.

Dorothea was delusional so some parts of her childhood have conflicting accounts. She states that she was the product of two alcoholic parents and that her mother was working as a prostitute before she died. She claimed her father was mentally unstable and often threatened to kill himself with a gun pointed to his head in front of the children (Dorothea would sometimes claim to be one of fourteen children.)

What is clear is that she was orphaned at the age of nine. Dorothea would then live in different orphanages, claiming to be sexually abused at one in particular. Eventually, her relatives from Fresno took her in. In her later years, she would discount the fourteen children claim and state that she was one of three children who were all born and raised in Mexico.

Dorothea would marry at the age of sixteen to a returning soldier named Fred McFaul. She would have two daughters a year later. Dorothea would give up both daughters, sending one to relatives in Sacramento and the other for adoption.

Dorothea would suffer a miscarriage in 1948 and McFaul would divorce her that same year. Angry at the failure of her marriage, she lied to everyone about the divorce and said that McFaul died of a heart attack shortly after their marriage ceremony.

She then turned to a life of crime. She would steal and forge checks. Dorothea would be caught in a forgery scam, serving six months of a one-year sentence. She would meet another man and become pregnant again. Dorothea would put the baby up for adoption as she hardly knew the man and could not afford the baby.

In 1952, she would marry a Swedish man named Axel Johansson.

CHOOSING A LIFE OF CRIME

Dorothea Puente would be married a total of four times with two documented divorces. She had another daughter which was put up for adoption at birth. The two would eventually meet, however, in 1986. Her daughter would describe her birth mother in unflattering terms, saying that she had "no real personality."

Dorothea would divorce Johansson in 1966 and marry Roberto Puente, a man that was almost twenty years her junior. The union would last only two years but Dorothea would keep his last name.

"Interesting that Dorothea would keep the last name of Puente," forensic psychologist Paula Orange said. "It became part of her con. She used the Spanish surname to con people into thinking that she was of Spanish descent. It helped her get some clients later on as she would use her surname as some kind of ethnic connection with them as in the case of the Costa Rican Bert Montalvo. She also cultivated a harmless old lady exterior in order to get people to put their guard down. She would tell people that she was seventy when in fact she was only fifty-nine. This con, this illusion would aid in her avoiding detection from social workers, parole agents and even the police."

Married life did not deter Dorothea's penchant for crime. Moving on from check forgery, she would run a brothel before being caught and arrested in 1960. Her sentence was relatively light, serving 90 days before being arrested for vagrancy and serving another three months.

Putting on a veneer that she was rehabilitated, Dorothea began working as a nurse's aide, providing care for physically disabled people and senior citizens in their private residences. This experience put a an idea in Dorothea's head.

She would manage boarding houses and cater to the elderly.

Dorothea finagled her way into becoming a manager for a three-story, 16-bedroom care home in Sacramento. She would marry for a fourth time, to a "raging drunk" named Pedro Montalvo. The union would only last a few months as Dorothea now took to trolling bars looking for older men who were receiving Social Security. She had the ability to put together tall tales, most often that she was a "famous actress" and told these men of her movie roles in films that didn't exist. In these movies, she always played the "evil woman." She also promoted herself as a "holistic doctor" and would listen intently to the maladies of her disabled mark before offering a suggestion on how they could improve their health. These stories would always lead to her convincing her mark to become one of her tenants after which she would steal their government check. She would talk a few into becoming her tenants the she would steal their government checks.

ARRESTS AND MORE ARRESTS

In 1982, Puente would be arrested for drugging and robbing people she would meet in bars. She would serve two and a half years in jail before she returned to her boarding house duties.

"Dorothea struck everyone as a harmless figure," Orange said. "So when she started the boarding house no one in their right mind would see her as a threat. They saw her as a sweet old lady. Her boarding house was spotless, inside and out. You could take a white glove, run your fingers across the furniture and not come up with a speck of dust."

Puente was a meticulous gardener and neighbors would describe her as being "very protective of her lawn."

"If somebody walked on her lawn," a neighbor said. "She'd cuss them in language that would make a sailor blush."

It would be this same year that the murders began. Dorothea had a friend named Ruth Monroe who began living with her but would die shortly after from a pharmaceutical drug overdose.

"She was sad," Puente told police when they came to investigate. "Very sad. Her husband was dying."

The police believed her and the death was ruled as a suicide.

"This is the occasion where Puente learned how to game the system," Orange said. "She learned that if there was no crime scene there was no crime. The police found Ruth Monroe dead and really had no choice but to declare it a suicide as there was no evidence that a murder had taken place. That was probably the farthest thing from the mind of the police. How could this sweet old lady be guilty of drugging up her best friend then smothering her with a pillow. She just didn't fit the profile."

Only a few weeks later, the police would return as a tenant named Malcom McKenzie would claim that Puente was drugging and taking money from him. Puente would be investigated and charged with theft. Sentenced to prison for five years, she began a pen-pal correspondence with a man named Everson Gillmouth, a 77-year-old retiree living in Oregon. Puente was then released after serving only three years of her sentence and found the smitten Gillmouth waiting for her.

They soon began making wedding plans, Gillmouth quickly opening a joint back account as they moved into an apartment in Sacramento together.

In November of 1985, Puente would hire a handyman named Ismael Florez to install some wood paneling in her apartment. She paid the handyman and threw in Gillmouth's 1980 Ford pickup as part of the payment.

"My boyfriend no longer needs it," Puente said. "I'm also wondering if you could build me a box. Say six feet by three feet by two feet. Just need to store some books and stuff."

Florez agreed and Puente would fill the box with her "stuff". She then hired Florez to help ship the nailed-shut box to a nearby storage depot. Puente accompanied Florez on the trip until they reached the Garden Highway in Sutter County. She then told Florez to dump the box into the Sacramento River.

"Its just junk," Dorothea said.

Months later, a fisherman would discover the box sitting on the bank of the river. Police would open the box to reveal a horrendously decomposed body of an elderly man.

Everson Gillmouth.

But it would be three years before police would be able to positively identify Gillmouth. Dorothea would continue to cash his social security checks. She would write his family on his behalf, stating that he was "sick" and could not contact them himself.

NEW BOARDING HOME, SAME RULES

Puente would rent a different boarding home from the Odorico family in what would later be infamously called the "F Street Boarding House."

Dorothea charmed the Odorico family, keeping the house spotless. They thought of her as family and referred to her as "tia" (Spanish for aunt). Despite being unlicensed and on parole, Dorothea was allowed to manage the place and supervise tenants.

But Dorothea's reputation grew in the community. She gave to charities and went out of her way to help certain people when it attended to her needs. She went to a charity ball and California Governor Jerry Brown stepped across the room to kiss her on the cheek.

The Governor then asked her to dance to the delight of onlookers.

In 1986, Puente would strike a deal with social worker Peggy Nickerson in an effort to provide a home for senior citizens on fixed incomes.

"She was the best the system had to offer," Nickerson said as she referred over nineteen elderly people to Puente in two years.

Dorothea would be a "Godsend" to social workers because she had no qualms about accepting troubled tenants, elderly and disabled people who could be abusive and addicted to drugs.

But Dorothea simply wanted their money. By having them as her boarders, she would collect their money first and pay them as she saw fit. Parole agents would come and talk to Dorothea. They would order Dorothea to stay away from her senior citizen clientele to no avail. Dorothea was never cited.

"The parole agents definitely dropped the ball," Orange said. "They are overwhelmed with work but it was almost as if they turned a blind eye. Here was a woman who had a criminal record of forging checks, running a brothel, and stealing Social Security checks from the elderly. Somehow, someway, she was allowed to run a boarding house. It boggles the mind really but shows you how each part of the social system had a piece of the puzzle but no one connected the dots."

Puente played good cop and bad cop to her tenants. There were some who said she was cheap and detailed instances where she withheld both their mail and their money. But there were others who said she could be kind and would praise her cooking.

Despite her philanthropic veneer, Dorothea had an autocratic personality. If one of her tenants showed up late for a meal, they would be denied food. She would send them away then make the other tenants "say Grace" before the meal.

She also did not drive and used a local tax driver to shuttle her around town.

"She had a lot of rules," Dorothea's driver Patty Rohrbach said. "Number one, be punctual. Number two, do what I tell you. And we'll get a long just great. She was generous almost to a fault. She'd tip very nicely and make sure there was enough time on the meter to make it worth my while."

Dorothea had a routine. She would go to the local hardware store to get gardening supplies, then get groceries. On Sundays, she would go to church then go to bars to solicit possible clientele.

"Dorothea would target the down and out," Orange said. "She would go to bars and offer a listening ear to someone who looked disabled or elderly. She knew how to game the system and would give the person tips on how to collect more on their Social Security or disability check. Then she would hand them her business card and invite them to stay with her as a boarder."

"She called them 'throwaway people,'" Rohrbach recalled. "She said 'everyone has abandoned them and I've taken them in.' And I thought it was a charitable situation created for people who had nowhere else to go."

Rohrbach wasn't the only one taken in by Dorothea's facade. Social worker Nickerson brought a man named Bert Montoya to live in Dorothea's boarding home. She had taken special interest in Montoya as the 50-year-old Costa Rican needed a place to stay desperately. He was an alcoholic schizophrenic, a man who constantly "heard voices in his head" but someone who Nickerson perceived as a "sweet, kind man."

"Montoya had been living in a place called 'Detox,'" Orange said. "A shack of a homeless shelter that had little more than vinyl mattresses on concrete."

Dorothea took to Montoya almost immediately, sensing he was a lost soul in a teddy bear's body. Montoya had a kind spirit, he once found over two hundred dollars at a homeless shelter and turned it in. He was troubled but not dangerous.

He was someone Dorothea could take advantage of.

Dorothea would take Montoya around the home and introduce him to the other residents. First there was John McCauley, a loud mouth drunk that did all of Dorothea's bidding. Second was Ben Fink, another alcoholic who despite being Jewish had a swastika tattoo on his arm. Lastly, there was John Sharpe, a compulsive gambler who suffered from short term memory loss.

"Dorothea took Bert Montoya under her wing," Orange said. "Moreso than the other tenants. He liked the fact that he could call her 'momma' and she called him her 'honey bear.' The social worker was surprised at how well he had adjusted to living under Puente's care. But Dorothea used him as a trophy. She used him to show everyone how compassionate and nurturing she could be."

The other tenants began getting jealous of Bert, in particular, John McCauley.

"The other tenants were paying upwards of $300 a month," Orange said. "They would get room and board plus two hot meals. Bert would get all that for free. All because Dorothea had taking a liking to the kind yet simple-minded man."

Dorothea went so far as to set up Bert with a running tab at the local bar. Bert would come in to the tavern, drink no more than three beers, then be on his way.

As much as Dorothea took to Bert as her showpiece, Ben Fink was a thorn in her side.

Fink would drunk himself into a stupor and had an uncanny ability to achieve alcohol levels that would be enough to kill an elephant, let alone a human being.

One night, the compulsive John Sharp was watching a horror movie in his room when he heard a large thump. The sound came from the upstairs bedroom that belonged to Ben Fink. Then he heard large bumps coming down the steps, as if someone were dragging a body. He thought it creepy at the time but didn't investigate.

Ben Fink would then disappear from the boarding house.

No one thought anything of it, however, as boarding house occupants were a transient group of people. Dorothea herself would kick people out after a few weeks and sometimes tenants themselves would leave on their own accord.

Dorothea never liked Ben Fink. Bert Montoya was until one night he did something to get into her doghouse.

Bert had went to the local tavern and this time he had gotten so drunk that he passed out inside the bar. Three of the other tenants had to carry him back to the boarding house.

"The group of men that brought him back described Bert as 'blowing bubbles' through his mouth," Orange said. "So that opens up the possibility that he had something else in his system aside from alcohol. We could easily surmise that Dorothea had begun to drug him up and the alcohol only exacerbated his symptoms. But something had spooked Bert. Something prompted him to drink more than his usual amount. He was trying to medicate himself and forget something he had seen at the boarding house."

Bert then ran away from the home, walking miles in order to return to 'Detox', the homeless shelter downtown.

"I don't want to go back," Bert cried out when the Detox manager allowed him back into the home. "I don't want to go back."

WHAT IS THAT SMELL?

Tenants in the boarding house began complaining about a rancid smell that was coming from the empty bedroom upstairs.

This would later be labeled as the "Death Room".

When the owners of the home, the Odoricos, came to do their monthly inspection they couldn't help but notice the odor themselves.

"It smelled rotten," Ricardo said. "It smelled rotten in there."

"I thought it was the tenants,"said Laura Arebalo, Ricardo's daughter. "because some tenants they would not bath on a daily basis."

Dorothea deflected the complaints as expected. She would blame the neighbors, saying they must be cooking something that's "not right." Then when that sounded lame she would blame a broken sewage line.

But late at night, Dorothea would shampoo the carpet in the room, awaking John Sharp.

When tenants and the owner asked about the room, Dorothea would simply say it was a room that was "cursed."

It was the same room where her friend Ruth Monroe had died only a few years earlier.

Neighbors complained to the city and the Department of Health was called in. They did an inspection of the house and made Dorothea sign a few documents.

But the smell remained.

And Bert Montoya returned.

After over two weeks on the streets and sleeping at "Detox" he arrived back at Dorothea's door steps.

Bert wanted to slip back into the house unnoticed but Dorothea saw him.

"When they cross me," Dorothea said. "They don't cross me a second time."

Then Bert disappeared.

"There was a reason why Bert didn't want to go back to the house to begin with," Orange said. "He openly told the people at the Detox that he didn't want to go back. I think he saw something there. Mostly likely he saw them disposing of a body. Chopping up a corpse. Something had freaked him out and Dorothea knew he would eventually say something."

"Bert had become a problem for Dorothea," Sacramento Police Detective Cabrera said. "He might even bring the police. She couldn't allow Bert to bring attention to her. She apparently felt that there was only one thing to do."

MORE SUSPICIONS

Neighbors began taking note of the strange doings of a man only known as "Chief."

Dorothea thought of Chief as the resident handyman of the boarding home. She had the man do odd jobs around place even though he was an alcoholic. Neighbors saw that Chief carted off dirt and junk away in a wheelbarrow after digging in the basement of the boarding home. He then tore down a garage in the backyard and put in fresh cement.

Then Chief disappeared.

And the owners weren't pleased that Dorothea had put in a concrete patio without any consent on their part.

"One time I went to the house," Ricardo Odorico said. "And I found a concrete patio."

"I used to have lots of roses," Veronica Odorico said. "I liked roses. Then I went and saw that everything was different. I said (to Dorothea) 'What happened? You took out the roses. She said 'I don't like roses.' I used to tell my husband he gave her too much freedom. He said it was to improve the house. I said I liked it better like I had it before."

By May of 1988, neighbors no longer complained of a smell coming from Dorothea's home. Now they were complaining of a stench coming from Puente's backyard. Dorothea dismissed their concerns, telling them that she was using "fish emulsion" to fertilize her soil.

"We couldn't stand it," one neighbor said. "There was a sick smell in the air, and there were lots of flies in the area."

In November, of that same year, social worker Nickerson would arrive at Puente's boarding house to do a welfare check on her tenant, Bert Montoya.

Montoya had been last seen in August and Dorothea would tell the police that the man had "gone home to Mexico."

"Dorothea gave this huge elaborate story," Orange said. "But the social worker knew that Montoya would not have picked up and left without notifying her. Smelling something fishy, she notified the police."

Police initially believed Dorothea's story but returned after Nickerson stated that another one of her clients went missing after being in Puente's care.

"Dorothea was accommodating when the police came to question her," Orange said. "They could not do anything without her permission. They couldn't search the premises or even come inside her house. But she was very polite and allowed one of the detectives to look around the home. He found some medicine vials that looked suspicious. They had names of different tenants on the vials but they were all in one drawer of Dorothea's. Then the asked if they could look around in the garden. To his amazement, Dorothea remained cooperative and said it was okay."

The police began digging up Dorothea's back yard. Initially, the dig did not go well. The police unearthed eggshells, food and other articles of garbage. They discovered some leather-like material, with the detective describing it as "very opaque, leathery."

One of the detectives dug further and came upon what he thought was a tree root. He pulled on the "root" and broke it away.

It turned out to be a human leg bone.

And the leather-like material turned out to be decomposed flesh.

The police then discovered the first of several corpses on November 11th, 1988. They found two more the next day.

"It wasn't uncommon for old Victorian homes to have human remains in the backyard," Orange said. "People have dug holes in their backyards and have found bones that date back to the early 1900s. There were occasions where folks didn't have enough money for a proper burial so they buried bodies in the backyard to save money. Initially, that is what the police took the bones for. A case of an old time burial."

But news quickly spread throughout the town and people lined up around the home to gawk. The crowd swelled so large that the police had to cordon off the street. Hot dog and t-shirt vendors began to show up to sell their wares. One of the t-shirts had an elderly grandmother holding up a shovel. The caption on the shirt read "I dig Sacramento."

Dorothea then inquired with Detective Cabrera that she was going to "go for a cup of coffee" at the hotel. Cabrera himself walked her to the hotel to ensure that no one harassed her on the way.

The detective returned to the site and within twenty minutes, he unearthed another body.

"Where's Dorothea?" his Lieutenant asked.

"Dorothea would pay a cab driver sixty dollars to take her to Stockton," Orange said. "From there, she took a bus to Los Angeles."

The police remained on the premises and continued to dig. Three days later, they would unearth seven bodies. They would identify Ben Fink by his swastika tattoo. Dorothy Miller, an elderly alcoholic would be identified as well as Betty Palmer.

"One of the more gruesome finds was that of Betty Palmer," Orange said. "She had her hands and feet chopped off as well as her head. Police searched far and wide for her different body parts to no avail. They dug and even checked under the crawlspace of the house. It is believed that Palmer was Dorothea's second victim and she was perfecting her technique, removing whatever evidence of identification she could."

THE AFTERMATH

The police continued to search the boarding house but found no other bodies. They still believed that other murders took place and Puente had used other means to dispose of her victims.

"We are getting a large number of calls from people with relatives who have stayed there," the Sacramento Police said in an official statement. "There are a lot more than seven names."

Twenty five tenants of Puente were missing and unaccounted for as the police did forensic work on the seven corpses.

Meanwhile, Dorothea Puente remained on the run.

The search began for Puente and by November 17th, she had been spotted in a Los Angeles bar. She had introduced herself to a patron as "Donna Johansson" and began questioning the man about his disability income. She offered to move in with him and fix him "Thanksgiving dinner" despite only meeting the man.

"She invited the man back to her hotel," Orange said. "He found her charming but declined. She got up and left and he's watching television in the bar. A news report comes on and he sees Dorothea is wanted for murder."

The bar patron called the LAPD and Dorothea was arrested at her hotel. Detective Cabrera and other officials from Sacramento Police arrived in Los Angeles to take her back.

"I'm sorry, Detective," Dorothea said while sipping on a cup of coffee.

"Dorothea, I knew if we dig we're going to find more," Cabrera said. "I know that. I know that."

"Well, I didn't put them there," Dorothea said. "I couldn't drag a body any place."

"I believe that. But I believe there's somebody else involved here."

Cabrera knew that there was a distinct possibility that Dorothea had an accomplice.

"Bert Montoya weighed about two-hundred and fifty pounds," Cabrera said. "How does a person that's five-foot-three, five-foot-four, one hundred and thirty-five pounds carry somebody like that."

Resident John McCauley was arrested and questioned by the police. He was later released for lack of evidence.

The police went on to believe that Dorothea had unknowing accomplices, employing her tenants to dig the holes. She would cut the body into pieces. For the pieces she needed help with, she would roll the body part up in carpet or plastic and have someone carry it out.

THE DEATH ROOM

In December of 1988, forensic police work had positively identified four more victims that were uncovered at the Puente boarding home. The victims were Bert Montoya, Vera Martin, Dorothy Miller and Leona Carpenter.

There was evidence to believe that Carpenter was buried alive.

"She (Leona) was put in the ground shallow," Cabrera said. "It appears that her legs, the victim kicked her legs up. And in doing so compacted the dirt around her legs forming a little bridge."

The mystery remained about the smell of the "Death Room". There were no remains found in the room.

Yet the smell never went away.

"One thing I'll never forget is when I pulled the carpet back," Cabrera continued. "When I pulled it back, the most grotesque odor came out and I knew that it was putrefying body fluids. The thing is there was other people living there. And it (burying the bodies) was based on opportunity. When was the best opportunity to put the people in the ground. So these bodies would have to lie there (in the room) until a period or a time when she could get them into the ground. I was in those graves. There was no odor. There as no smell. But in the 'Death Room', the carpet. The body fluid had a smell that would knock you over....This was nothing more than a house of horrors."

THE MOTIVATION

The sum total of Puente's scheming and killing netted her more than $5,000 per month. In turn, she would take the clothing of her victims and donate them to charities.

"We would get calls from local charities," Cabrera recalled. "And they said they were given bags of clothing from Dorothea. Well, what a great way to get rid of evidence."

Dorothea would be brought to trial and prosecutors would describe her as one of the most "cold, calculating" serial killers in American history. No one ever witnessed her kill anybody but Dorothea would later reveal that she would use drugs to overdose her victims. Forensics would discover traces of a prescription strength sleeping pill in all of the remains.

The social security checks would continue to arrive at the residence despite the tenant being deceased.

Dorothea used part of her ill-gotten gains to get a facelift.

On December of 1993, Dorothea would be convicted on three counts of murder of the nine bodies discovered.

"The tragedy in looking back at this story is that it could have been prevented," Orange said. "No one took the time to investigate Dorothea's background. Different agencies knew different information about her yet no one collaborated. The true victims are, of course, the deceased. They were referred to Dorothea as the 'throwaway people'. People that when she dumped into the ground, no one came looking. The tragedy is that Dorothea was right. But for the circumstances surrounding the disappearance of Bert Montoya, who knows how many more murders she would have committed?"

She was sentenced to life in Chowchilla State Prison and she died in 2011.

DEATH ROW GRANNY

Georgia Johnson

It never ends.

No way.

No way am I letting this man demean and degrade me another day.

He's just like my father.

A binge drinker. And the binges were happening more and more.

He's on the road to nowhere and taking me with him.

It never ends.

First my father. Now him.

Fuck it.

I threw the cigarette on the blanket. I knew it was flammable.

Then I watched the smoke rise and smiled.

In Lumberton, North Carolina, Thomas Burke fell victim to a house fire which was caused by a burning cigarette. Investigative authorities thought that he had fallen asleep while smoking, leaving thirty-eight-year-old Velma Burke as his widow.

They didn't know that the fire was set by Velma.

Velma knew how to play the part of the grieving widow. She cried and gave the authorities the requisite crocodile tears. No one would believe that the murder of Thomas Burke would set off a series of killings performed by the seemingly kind and harmless church-going woman with the soft voice.

But Velma was a killer...

EARLY LIFE

Velma Bullard grew up as the second of nine children in the rural part of Sampson County, North Carolina.

Times were tough for the Bullard family. They would live on a small farm with no electricity, running water or an outhouse.

"They had to go outdoors," forensic psychologist Paula Orange said. "The entire family had to endure the indignity of going into the woods or using pots to shit and piss."

The home was small and cramped for the nine children. Velma would be forced to sleep in the same bedroom with her parents until the age of five.

Her father was a loom repairman (fixing an apparatus that was used to weave clothing) and an abusive alcoholic. Velma had an older brother, Olive, who were subject to his nightly beatings. Lillie, her mother, was too meek to protect her children from her husband's violent outbursts.

"She had the type of father who would not need any provocation," Orange said. "He would take out the pettiest frustrations, like not being able to find something around the house, and take it out on the children. Velma would become resentful toward her mother who was too weak or indifferent to stop her father from beating on the kids. She accepted his discipline as 'the way it was.'"

Velma would find school as a welcome escape from her dreadful home life. She loved her teacher and was an excellent student during her early grade school years. When she would return home from school, she took solace in the fact that her father would always arrive home late as he worked long hours at the textile mill.

"Her father Murphy had that Protestant work ethic in him," Orange said. "He accepted the long hours and low pay, seeing a kind of nobility in that. Only problem was, he would binge drink. Not store bought alcohol but homemade moonshine. After a couple of shots, he would be 'lit' and inflict his wrath on everyone in the house."

By the age of eleven, Velma would be forced to take on various chores around the farm. She would clean up the house, washing and iron everyone's clothing (eleven people). Her father would chastise her for not mending or sewing his work clothes properly as well.

"Her father was a stern taskmaster," Orange said. "Hell, you can say 'slave driver.' He would have Velma come home early from school days when the laundry got too backed up. Velma hated this and felt embarrassed. Her family didn't have much and as she grew older her classmates began to see her for what she was, a poor girl that was an easy mark for teasing."

Velma would grow to be 5'3" but gain weight as she got older. She would be mocked about her obesity, her shoddy clothes the gap between her two front teeth. She would also be called "knot head" after she ran head first into a boy at school which left a permanent contusion on her forehead.

By the age of twelve, Velma seemed to have taken on all of her mother's duties. She would cook all of the family meals in addition to performing cleaning around the farm house. She would miss school for days at a time as her father forced her to complete chores around the home before she could continue her education.

"Academic achievement was not at the forefront of her father's mind," Orange said. "Her mother was of little use because of her depression and mental illness. Velma was the oldest girl so she took on the duties of mom at an age where she should have been playing with dolls."

ANGER, ABUSE, AND CHURCH

Despite her father's verbal abuse and alcohol-fueled beatings, the family kept up a face of religious interest. Velma would be sent to Bible school every year until the age of thirteen. During her last year of Bible school, her father marked the occasion by buying Velma a silk pink dress with ribbons. Velma recalled the day as one of the happiest of her life.

The happiness would be short-lived.

Velma would claim that her father raped her when she was thirteen years old. She revealed this only to her pastor in her later years before she stood trial. Velma did not even tell her mother whom she did not think would believe the molestation took place.

"Things that went on inside our home when I grew up," Velma said. "Were kept inside."

At the age of fifteen, Velma continued to excel in school. Despite her chubby physique, she becomes adept at basketball and is pegged to be the team's star player for the upcoming season. But her father did not allow her to play.

"Who is going to iron these damn clothes?" he snarled.

The family then moved to Robeson county and switched from the Presbyterian denomination to Baptist. It was here that Velma would meet Thomas Burke and the two made it clear that they wanted to date. Once again, Velma's father would intervene, telling Velma that she had to wait until her sixteenth birthday until she could date.

The two waited patiently for her birthday to arrive and the following year Thomas would propose to her while they went to the movies.

Knowing that her father would not approve, Velma and Thomas eloped, moving to Dillon, South Carolina. Neither Thomas or Velma had any money as they both quit high school to get married. Thomas then went to work at a local textile mill.

"At this point, I believe that Velma began to realize that her life would not be that much better with Thomas," Orange said. "He literally has the same job as her father."

Economics forced Velma and Thomas to move in with his parents. This arrangement would last for a year until Thomas got a better paying job at a soft drink company.

At the age of nineteen, Velma would give birth to her first son, Ronnie. The couple would then move back to Parkton, North Carolina where they would remain in the same home for eleven years. Two years later, the young couple would welcome a daughter named Kim.

A CYCLE OF RELIGION AND ABUSE

The Burkes would be fixtures at the local Baptist church with Velma taking the reigns to teach a Sunday school class. But the prayers and sermons would do little to offset the growing ennui in the Burke home. Two years after giving birth to Kim, Velma would get hit by a drunk driver while crossing the street. She would be hospitalized for an extended period, suffering both physically and mentally.

Thomas' job at the soft drink company would not be enough to provide for the family. Velma would be forced to leave her small children at home and work in a textile mill just like her father. The couple would have different work hours, with Velma working nights and Thomas working days as they would take turns watching the children.

Velma would fall victim to the hard work at the mill and the stress of raising two young children. She began bleeding and her doctor performed a hysterectomy.

Velma's mother would take pity on the couple and give them one acre of land near their old farm. Thomas would build a three-bedroom home for the family but Velma was already going down a slippery slope. Her personality changed after the hysterectomy, claiming that she always felt "nervous and afraid."

Things would get worse as Thomas suffered a head injury in a car accident. He then began to drink heavily and begin to beat Velma.

"It was deja vu," Orange said. "Velma had, in essence, married her father."

One night, the couple argued and Thomas punched Velma in an alcohol-fueled tantrum. The police are called to the home and Velma sent Thomas to the state hospital to get treatment for his drinking. Her husband remains there for three days but when he returns home, his behavior is worse than behavior. He's angry at Velma for sending him to the "drunk tank". His alcoholism worsens and he would go on to lose his job because of absenteeism.

"Velma is thirty-five years old at this time," Orange said. "But she's an old thirty-five with crow's feet under her eyes and a hangdog look. She's had a rough life, not necessarily by her own design, and it has taken its toll."

Velma leaves the textile mill but then finds two different jobs in order to support the family. During the day, she works as a sales clerk in a Belk department store. At night, she goes to work as a machine operator in a cotton mill.

Thomas, meanwhile, would continue to drink.

He rages on a daily basis, on one occasion he pinned son Ronnie up against the wall and threatened him with a knife. Velma would faint during the encounter and be transported to the hospital. She was diagnosed as having a nervous breakdown and lapsed into a serious depression. The medical staff gave her tranquilizers to calm down. Velma believed that it was during this stint in the hospital that she became addicted to the painkillers.

"The drugs were helping," Orange said. "When nothing else did. So she wanted more and more."

Velma's children acknowledged that their mother's mood swings were due to the drugs.

Over the next three years, Velma would go in and out of the hospital for drug overdoses. After each visit, her addiction only grew as did her prescription list.

"She fell through the cracks in her own family," Orange said. "And in the system itself. Her family had their own issues to deal with as Thomas would abuse everyone on a daily basis. Finally, Velma did something she could control. She killed her husband."

On April 21st, 1969, Velma would drop a cigarette on the floor of her home and waited until her husband inhaled enough smoke to die.

His death, however, would do nothing to solve Velma's problems.

Her addictions and anxiety would only get worse.

A HOSPITAL FREQUENT FLYER

Velma would have another nervous breakdown after killing Thomas and lapse into a guilt-ridden depression. But seven months later, a co-worker at the Belk department store would introduce her to fifty-four-year-old Jennings Barfield. Jennings had emphysema and diabetes but Velma would marry him anyway. Unlike her marriage with Thomas which started out well, Velma's marriage with the older Jennings would be troubled from the start. Her drug addiction would escalate and Jennings would express his own regret at marrying her.

"I don't know why I married her," Jennings said. "All she does is pop pills all day."

After less than three years of marriage, Velma decided to part ways with Jennings. She didn't file for divorce, however, she decided to poison him with arsenic. She would later claim that she only meant to "make him sick."

Jennings Barfield was already ill and doctors had no suspicion that Velma was behind the death. Arsenic was a slow burn poison that could kill without detection. The autopsy called for no arsenic test and Velma had gotten away with murder once again.

But Seven months later, Velma would overdose on her prescription meds and become hospitalized. Her family recognized the pattern but could not wean Velma off of the drinks. She would remain hospitalized for three weeks.

Her personality seemed to change after the hospital release. She returned to work at Belk department store but kept being combative and argumentative with customers. Her boss knew of her circumstances and tried to coax her to do better. He took her away from the public contact and into the back stock room where he had her put pricing on the clothing items.

Her boss soon realized that Velma's addiction had gotten out of control. Velma would not be able to function in the back room, leaving tasks uncompleted as she would have her prescription medications delivered to the store.

"It is a hopeless situation," the store manager told Velma's son Ronnie before he fired his mother.

BROKE AND DESTITUTE

With no income, Velma would lose the family home as she no longer paid the mortgage. She would be forced to move back in with her parents and face the two people she blamed everything for.

Her father had grown ill, however, and would die from lung cancer shortly after Velma moved back into the home. She would feel bad about her father's death and admit that she had a love/hate relationship with him.

"I had learned to love him as much as I had hated him," Velma said. "He was so good to my kids. I think he tried to do with my kids like he wished he had done to us. He could not stand to see me correct them. If I would pick them up and spank them, he would ask me, 'Isn't that enough?'"

But after her father's death Velma self-medicated once again. She overdosed and was hospitalized for two weeks. Her family didn't judge, they instead thought she was "cursed."

"Velma needed psychiatric help," Orange said. "So she began medicating herself with deleterious results. She would "doctor shop" for different physicians who would be manipulated into giving her the drugs she wanted. Her addiction eventually grows until she becomes desperate for money in order to fuel the drug habit."

A MURDERER AND A THIEF

Velma began stealing from those closest to her, starting with her mother. Her mother confronted Velma about a missing check and Velma went ballistic.

"She had violent mood swings," Orange said. "The medication had completely changed her personality as she needed the drugs above all else. The people around her were not familiar with how to handle a person who had this kind of mental illness. So this made for a very dangerous cocktail for her and anyone close to her."

Hitting a new low, Velma took out a $1,000 loan under her mother Lillie's name. She put up the family home as collateral and forged her mother's signature on the documents. Velma then blew through the money and a month later took out another loan, once again using her mother's house as collateral. The following month, she emptied the checking account on her now deceased husband, Jennings. Two months later, the loan company began sending Velma overdue notices as she had not been paying off the loan.

"In Velma's mind," Orange said. "She had no other choice but to kill off her own mother."

Velma went to the local pharmacy and looked for bottles that had the warning of "fatal if ingested." She put the poison into a drink for her mother and watched as she drank the fatal elixir.

Her mother then began vomiting and lost control of her bowels. Within a few hours, her mother could not so much as walk and an ambulance was called.

Velma came to visit her in the hospital to finish the job. Armed with a Thermos, she made a special concoction of chicken soup and arsenic.

"Drink it slow," Velma said as she tenderly lifted the cups to the lips of her ailing mother. "Slow."

Her mother would eventually die of "natural causes" as no one suspected Velma of committing murder. Instead, she received sympathy.

"So sorry for your loss," hospital staff said.

"The thing with arsenic is that it shuts down the whole system," Orange said. "So hospital staff just chalked up her mother's weakness to old age. Checking for arsenic poisoning would be the furthest thing from their mind."

Velma showed the necessary emotion and received sympathy from friends and family. She then moved in with her daughter Kim and son-in-law Dennis who lived in a trailer park. She could not evade the authorities for long though as the authorities caught wind of Velma's check forgeries.

Velma reacted as she always did. She would run away and medicate herself.

"Her drug addiction kept pushing her into a corner and she saw no way out," Orange said. "So, this time, she goes to her son Ronnie's house and overdoses again, trying to kill herself. She falls and breaks her collar bone which laid her out in the hospital another three weeks."

But the police find her situation unsympathetic.

"We're sorry, Velma," the deputy informed her at her hospital bed. "But once you have been cleared for release, we will arrest you."

Velma would not have that. She tried to overdose again but this go around the hospital staff pumped out her stomach.

She was sent to court the next day and sentenced to six months in jail for the forgery. She is released after four months for good behavior.

NO REHAB HERE

Her addiction still unchecked, Velma returned to live with Kim and her son-in-law. She rummaged through the belongings of her son-in-law and stole a check, forging his name so she can get more prescription meds. Her daughter Kim now has caught wind of her mother's addiction, pleading with her doctors to stop prescribing her.

"In some ways," Orange said. "The doctors were just as guilty as she was. But back in the day, there was no way to cross-reference this stuff like we do now. Once she had her fill with one doctor she would go to the next and the next."

Velma's addiction prevented her from taking a forty-hour a week job. So she looked for alternative forms of income.

She would find a job taking care of the elderly.

Montgomery and Dolly Edwards would be her first clients.

"She found herself some easy targets," Orange said. "There didn't seem to be any legislative body in place that prevents sociopaths from caretaking the elderly. So Velma doesn't slip through any cracks, she just befriends the elderly couple and begins taking care of them."

Montgomery was blind and unable to walk. He was 93-years old and his 83-year old wife was too feeble to take care of him. They paid $75 a week for Velma to become their live-in caretaker.

All was good, at least in the beginning. But Dolly had a sharp tongue and would criticize Velma daily. Velma would keep a nice exterior unless confronted, saw Dolly has yet another wheel in her cycle of verbal abuse.

"It seemed to be a never-ending loop for her," Orange said. "Being forced to deal with verbally abusive people. Velma had long since snapped and Dollie simply had no idea who she was dealing with."

Velma began to plot out Montgomery and Dollie's demise until she meets their nephew, Stuart Taylor.

Stuart was already married but was blown away when he met the caretaker of his Aunt Dollie.

Velma would play it cool, stealing what she could from the couple in terms of petty cash and household items that had value. They outlived their usefulness to her within a year as Montgomery died of "natural causes". One month later, Dolly also passed away.

And again, no one suspected the sweet and soft-spoken Velma to have had anything to do with their deaths.

MOVING ON

Velma saw being a caretaker as a perfect front for her. She could steal as much money as she could and when the old folks detected something amiss she would simply poison them. After killing the Edwards' couple, she set the word out at church that she as available to be a caregiver. The pastor would refer her to Margie Lee Pittman who was seeking for a caregiver for her elderly parents, John Henry and Record Lee.

"She comes here twice a week," the pastor reassured Pittman. "She's a nice, kindly woman. You can't go wrong."

Pittman's father, John Henry Lee, was eighty years old when he discovered that his new caregiver had forged a $50 check on his account. He then fell violently ill, suffering through a spastic spell of vomiting, diarrhea, and convulsions. The doctors would chalk up his quick death to gastroenteritis but in fact, he had been poisoned with arsenic.

Velma played the caregiver role until his end. She attended his funeral and cried with the family, sending an ornate wreath (with money stolen from the dead man) to the proceedings.

For whatever reason, Velma spared Lee's wife and moved back to Lumberton, North Carolina to live in a trailer park. She began working as an aide in a nursing home and received word from Stuart that he was now a widow. The two began dating and she moved part of her belongings into his home.

"Stuart is a nice guy," Orange said. "He has no idea what kind of woman Velma is. She is so manipulative and cunning that the younger man is putty in her hands. So the relationship starts great as she reels him in with kindness and charm."

The couple are happy cohabitating until Stuart Stuart finds a letter addressed to Velma from the state penitentiary.

Curious, he began reading the correspondence and realized that is from a former cellmate of Velma.

Stuart became enraged. He threatened to "expose" Velma to all of his family and friends. Somehow, someway, however, she was able to calm him down.

He then found out that she had forged over $200 in checks on his account. The two argued but stayed together for the next two months.

"Velma had the Christian facade down pat," Orange said. "She asked Stuart to forgive her and the next thing you know they are going to a Rex Humbard revival. But before they went, she poured arsenic poison in both his beer and tea. She made sure he drank every drop."

Returning home from the revival, Stuart started to vomit on the drive home, the poison kicking in.

Velma had to keep the con going. She had to appear like a concerned girlfriend so she called up Stuart's daughter, Alice, later that night and told her that Stuart had came down with the flu.

Stuart's daughter expressed concern but Velma kept her at bay.

"Don't you worry now, honey. I'll take care of everything."

Stuart died the next day.

Velma would speak at Stuart's funeral and tearfully asked for his wedding band. His family graciously allowed her to have it and gave her $400 to help her cope with the grief.

But Alice knew her father was a picture of health. She vociferously argued for more tests beyond the standard autopsy and sure enough, arsenic had been found in Stuart's tissues.

On March 10th, 1978, the sheriffs arrived at Velma's home to bring her in for questioning. She was interrogated for over three hours, holding her ground. But she knows the evidence will trump her denials and tries to commit suicide after being released. This go around, however, her son Ronnie stopped her.

The sheriffs come to visit Velma again and she has one more surprise up her sleeve.

But Velma has one more surprise up her sleeve.

She would confess. Not only for the murder of Stuart but of six others.

"I set my first husband on fire," Velma confessed without an attorney present. "And I killed the rest of them."

"It was almost as if she wanted to be free of the guilt she had been carrying," Orange said. "Her confession seemed to take a burden off her back."

"The last ten years were like that," Velma said. "A drug nightmare. It was a case of not knowing where you are or what you've done."

The bodies of her victims were later exhumed and all tested positive for arsenic.

FACING THE GRIM REAPER

Velma's case would be prosecuted by Joe Freeman Britt, who was listed in the Guinness Book of World Records as the country's "deadliest prosecutor."

Velma would plead not guilty by reason of insanity but the court denied her plea.

"I needed to keep them sick until I could pay back the money I had stolen from them," Velma said. "I wanted to earn their thanks by nursing them back to health. I needed the money. I was addicted to pain killers. Anti-depressants. Amphetamines."

On November 23rd, 1978, Velma's trial would begin in Elizabethtown, North Carolina where she would be charged with the first-degree murder of her boyfriend, Stuart Taylor. The trial lasted seven days and the jury reached a verdict of guilty, placing her on death row at the age of 47. She was scheduled to be executed on February 3rd, 1979 but received a stay.

Velma would be sentenced to death and the verdict was appealed all the way to the U.S. Supreme court. Her attorney maintained that the jury had never been presented with the full extent of Velma's "addiction and background." Velma remained tight-lipped about that to everyone but her pastor. Her attorney felt thought her horrific background could have been used as part of her defense and the jury would have found her to be more of a sympathetic case.

CHANGING SPOTS?

"She's not the same person who went to prison in 1978," Kim Burke Norton, Velma's daughter said.

While in jail, Velma became a model prisoner.

"The first week I was here was the worst week," Velma recalled. "Everything about it."

Velma no longer had access to her drugs in prison and she began to dry out. With daily visits from two different pastors, Velma began to discuss her anger and repressed issues that fueled her addiction and murders.

Velma would claim that as she was awaiting trial in 1978 she came to a "meeting with Christ" that caused her to "change inwardly."

Velma heard a broadcast by radio evangelist JK Kinkle. "Jesus loves you, prisoners, too," Kinkle said. "He died for you too. No matter what you've done, the Lord will forgive you."

After Velma heard this sermon, she dropped to her knees and cried out to God.

She would then become the "go to" counselor for young inmates in the prison.

The inmates would nickname Velma as "Mama Margie" because of her wisdom and she would in turn think of them as her "adopted children."

The prison guards and counselors would take the most incorrigible prisoners and place them in a cell next to Velma. Velma would invariably counsel the young prisoner and advise them on the correct path.

"They'd come in ready to kill themselves," Sister Mary Teresa Floyd said. "And here she was with a death sentence, mothering and helping them."

"Living in prison is a struggle," Velma said. "Even at its best. And I know that without Him and His strength that has sustained me, I couldn't have made it even this far."

Her stay on death row soon became a part of the news brief. During this time, a phalanx of evangelists would take her cause to the mainstream. The Reverend Hugh Hoyle would become Velma's personal minister as she received stays of execution in September, October and December of 1981. She would also have a letter correspondence with Ruth Graham, Billy Graham's wife as well as meeting their daughter Ann.

While Velma impressed the Christian do-gooders, the family members of the victims were not taken in by her "conversion."

"She's got religion now, they say," Margie Lee Pittman said. "Well, she had religion before. So we all thought."

A few more stays were granted until 1984 when the U.S. Supreme Court justice Warren Burger granted her a stay until August of that year. At this point, however, her execution seemed inevitable. In an ironic move, Velma would choose poison rather than the gas chamber and enjoyed the final visits from her children and grandchildren.

During the final week before her execution, the Reverend Hoyle, and his wife came to the prison with a battery-powered portable keyboard. His wife played the little organ then the Reverend sang "He Hideth My Soul" and "He is So precious to Me" in the cramped visitor booth.

Velma sang along, whistling in the graveyard before the reaper came for her.

She then wrote letters to each of the victim's family asking them for forgiveness. Reverend Hoyle would deliver the letters to the families, all of whom would refuse them.

MEET THE HANGMAN

As her execution date neared, Velma was placed in a solitary cell that stood directly across from the death chamber.

"It's total isolation," Velma said. "From everyone I had been with for six years."

North Carolina Governor James B.Hunt would reject her final plea for clemency.

On the day of her execution, the jail house would turn into a media frenzy. Death penalty advocates gathered outside the prison and chanted "Hip, hip, hurrah...K-I-L-L" while some sloganeered with "burn, bitch, burn". The protesters held up a few placards that quote Romans ch.13 which ironically was a verse that Velma would repeat to guards during her prison stay.

"For rulers are not a terror to good works, but to the evil...(The ruler) beareth no the sword in vain, for he is the minister of God, a revenger to execute wrath upon him that doeth evil."

The execution was scheduled to take place at 2:00 a.m but the protesters remained outside, their chants reduced to a simple "Kill her! Kill her!"

On November 2nd, 1984, Velma would be executed by lethal injection. The prison official came out and addressed the press, giving out copies of Barfield's statement of apology. The reporters then eagerly anticipated what Velma requested for her last meal. Initially, Velma just wanted the normally scheduled prison food; chicken livers, collard greens and a sheet cake with peanut butter icing. The last meal was delivered but Velma immediately lost her appetite. Instead, she opted for Cheese Doodles and a glass of Coca-Cola.

"Her attorney believed that Velma could have done some good in life," Orange said. "He stated that she could have become a teacher, counselor or a pastor. But her father set her on a path of self-destruction that she couldn't escape from. By the time she the left that road to ruin, she was too far gone in terms of her murderous acts. Justice had to be served in the end. In the end, the law doesn't care how genuine you are in your pleas for forgiveness. It only cares about the rule of law."

"I'm sorry for the hurt that I've caused," Velma said before her execution. "So many people, today if it were possible, I wish I could take every bit of hurt on myself."

THE MURDER OF BROOKE WILBERGER

OLIVIA WATSON

Chapter 1

May 24, 2004 is a day many people in Corvallis, Oregon will never forget. It was the day a drunk man who was also high on crack set forth to destroy a life. Joel Courtney set out that morning in his 1997 green Dodge Caravan in search of a young, pretty co-ed to fulfill his dark fantasies. He cruised through the Oregon State University campus, searching, failing. But Courtney was persistent, and his wishes were soon fulfilled after he came across the Oak Park apartment complex a block down the road.

On the same morning, Brooke Wilberger woke up without any inclination that this might be her final day on Earth. She was newly home after finishing her first year of University, and was enjoying how sunny the spring had turned out to be. She headed over to the Oak Park apartment complex, which her sister managed, to help do some cleaning and basic repairs. Her sister needed help washing the lightposts out in the parking lot, so Wilberger grabbed some rags and a bucket of soapy water and got to work.

A few minutes into her work, Wilberger noticed a green van pull up. Inside, a man was waving an envelope at her, trying to get her attention. He looked like he needed help, so Wilberger approached. When the van pulled away seconds later, all that was left of Brooke was the soapy water and her now-broken flip flops.

It would be more than five years before Brooke Wilberger came home, but she would never come home alive. The story of her disappearance was a twisted tale full of hope, but it would only ever have a bittersweet ending.

Chapter 2

Brooke Wilberger was born in Fresno, California on February 20, 1985. She was the youngest of six. With three older sisters and two older brothers, she lived in a busy household, but it was a pleasant place to live. Her parents, Greg and Cammy Wilberger, were devout Mormons, and raised their children to be the same. The family was incredibly close-knit.

Brooke Wilberger grew to be quite a beautiful, accomplished young woman. Besides boasting a strong set of mormon morals, she also excelled in school and had a lot of friends. The tall, thin blonde also received a lot of attention from the guys in her school, but she seldom dated.

The summer before Brooke began high school, the Wilberger family left California behind and moved North to Eugene, Oregon. Here, Brooke attended Elmira High School, and met her first serious boyfriend, Justin Blake. Blake also came from a mormon family, and was devoted to his religion, so the couple got along famously. They respected each other's minds, bodies, and faith.

The young couple graduated together in 2003, and while they were both dedicated to each other, they were on different paths towards the future. Wilberger wanted to go right to college so she could better equip herself with the knowledge she would need to turn around and better those in need around her. Blake was ready to jump into missionary work.

Wilberger was accepted into the Brigham Young University in Provo, Utah, and when she set off for her freshman year there, Blake set off for Venezuela to participate in a Mormon missionary campaign.

Although she was separated from her first love, Wilberger could not deny how happy she was at Brigham Young. The University was owned and operated by the Church of Jesus Christ of Latter Day Saints, and was the largest religious university in the country. She was immersed in her faith in new experiences and knowledge. She was actively participating in something much larger than herself, and she loved it.

Wilberger kept in constant contact with her family while away at University. She would often call and tell them about what she was learning, who she was meeting, and what she was doing. Her favorite topic of conversation, though, was always the inspiration her surroundings gave her to do better for the world. Although she was excited to see her family after the end of the year, she was in no rush to leave the busy, bustling campus for small-town Oregon.

After finishing her classes for the year, Brooke returned home to her family in late April of 2004. Her parents still lived in Eugene, but she wanted to maintain some of her freedom, so Brooke often stayed with her sister, Stephanie, who lived an hour outside of Eugene in an apartment complex she managed in Corvallis.

Her family were ecstatic to have her back home, close by, where they believed she would be safe.

Chapter 3

On May 24, 2004, Brooke had been home for about a month. She was staying with her sister in the Oak Park apartments, which were just down the road from Oregon State University, where summer classes were already in full swing.

That morning, a female student of Oregon State named Randy was walking through the Reser Stadium parking lot when she noticed a green van driving around her. When it pulled up next to her, the driver of the van got out and asked Randy for directions. The student had a bad feeling about the man, and when she looked in the back seat of the van she noticed a bunch of empty boxes and blankets. Before the man could get too close, Randy excused herself and hurried off to class.

Several minutes later, another student, Crystal, was approached by the same van in the same parking lot. Crystal did speak to the man, who again asked for directions, but the conversation was interrupted by an athletic's coach, who Randy had reported the earlier incident to. When confronted by the coach, the van's driver quickly jumped back into his vehicle and sped off of the campus.

While this was all happening, Brooke Wilberger was a block down the road from Reser Stadium at the Oak Park apartment complex. That morning she was planning on helping her sister Stephanie do some routine maintenance work on the complex. She decided to start with washing the lamp posts in the parking lot, so she grabbed a bucket, filled it with soapy water, and headed outside. Stephanie saw Brooke hard at work scrubbing the lamp posts at 10:00 a.m. It was the last time she ever saw her sister alive.

Shortly after 10:00 a.m., the same green van that had been causing havoc on the Oregon State campus pulled into the Oak Park apartment complex. The van pulled up to Brooke, blocking her view of the apartments. He began asking for directions, but when Brooke drew near, he pulled out a knife and forced the 19-year-old into the back seat of his van and sped away.

Five minutes down the road, the van pulled over and it's driver, Joel Courtney, got out and bound Wilberger's arms and legs with duct tape. He also covered her body with blankets he had stashed in the back seat. After this, he sped off towards a nearby area that was covered with heavy forestation.

Hours after Brooke was snatched from the apartment complex, her sister Stephanie realized that she hadn't seen or heard from her in a while. She decided to track her down to make sure she was okay, and began with the place she had last seen her—the complex's parking lot. When she got there she was surprised to see an almost empty parking lot, save for the cleaning supplies Brooke had been using and Brookes flip flop sandals, one of which was now broken.

Stephanie immediately ran inside and called police, who immediately launched a missing person's case despite their protocol stating they should wait 24-hours first. Brooke's broken flip flops at her last known location triggered enough of an alarm.

When detectives arrived at the Oak Park apartments, they quickly discovered that her truck, purse, phone, and wallet were all still at the apartments. If she had left the apartments by herself, she had done so without any identification, money, and shoes. It seemed unlikely that this would have been the case.

The search for Brooke began in the same way most crimes do—with the victim's significant other. In this case, Brooke's long-term boyfriend was quickly eliminated because he was over 4000 miles away doing missionary work in Venezuela. Brooke's family was also quickly ruled out.

During this process, the word of Brooke's disappearance quickly got out to the community, and a massive volunteer search was launched by the Wilberger's Mormon church. Within days of Brooke's disappearance, both Eugene and Corvallis were covered in missing posters detailing Brooke's physical appearance and last known location. Over 4000 acres of heavily-wooded area outside of Corvallis was searched for any signs of the missing girl over eleven days. None were found.

Police soon began to realize that the best chance they had of finding Wilberger would be to find the person who had taken her from the Oak Park apartments, so they quickly began to focus on the few early leads they had in the case.

The method in which Wilberger was abducted led police to believe that her abductor was a repeat offender. It's difficult to grab a grown woman off of the streets without anyone seeing or hearing anything. Police began looking through sex offender registries and crime logs to create a suspect pool, one that turned out to include over one thousand names, all of whom were interviewed.

One of the first people contacted by police was 45-year-old ex-con Lauren Hugo Krueger. He had been convicted in 1985 for attempted rape and had served time for the felony assault and kidnapping of a 23-year-old jogger. Krueger had also been questioned in relation to several reports of harassment and stalking. Most damningly, Krueger had also been spotted at a car dealership less than a block away from where Wilberger was abducted from. It was a promising start to the investigation.

Chapter 4

Many police officers in Corvallis believed they may have identified the man who abducted Brooke Wilberger on May 24, 2004, as being Lauren Krueger. He had committed several similar crimes in the past, making him a likely suspect. However, when he was interviewed, police discovered he had an airtight alibi for that afternoon, and he was eliminated in the case.

Shortly after Krueger was eliminated as a suspect, another man by the name of Sun Koo King was identified as a probably suspect. King was an Oregon State graduate who was unemployed and lived in the area. He had recently had a lot of trouble with the law for breaking and entering into Oregon State dorm rooms and stealing their occupants underwear.

Detectives searched King's home and found a startling collection of women's underwear, used tampons, and pubic hair. King also catalogued where he found each object of his collection, which allowed investigators to see that he had gotten most of the items from dorms at the University and from the laundry room at the Oak Park apartments, the same apartments Brooke Wilberger lived in with her sister.

Police were shocked by what they found at King's home, but what shocked them more was that there seemed to be no sign of Brooke Wilberger anywhere. Further, King passed a polygraph test and seemed to have an airtight alibi. Investigators were again forced to abandon the promising lead.

By October 2004, five months after Brooke's disappearance, police had a third strong suspect—Aeryn Evans. Evans had been arrested the month before for attacking a Oregon State student on campus. Evans' step sister called police after the incident suspecting that he may have been involved in Wilberger's disappearance too, but this was quickly discovered to be impossible by police.

Frustrated by having to eliminate three great suspects in a row, police decided they needed to take a different approach in the hunt for Wilberger's abductor. They decided to focus in on the one piece of evidence they had directly connected to the person who took Brooke—a green Dodge Caravan.

Police suspected that the green van was connected to Brooke's disappearance because of the two earlier reports from Randy and Crystal on the Oregon State campus, as well as from a tip call from a man who identified himself as Brian. Brian told police that he had seen a green van driving around the area Brooke was last seen. The driver was acting suspicious enough that the van had stood out to the man. The three incidents were too bizarre for police not to connect with Brooke's disappearance on the same day.

Both Randy and Crystal were interviewed by police, but neither were able to give a clear description of the van's driver. They had both been too spooked at the time. However, the coach that had intervened in Crystal's encounter with the van had gotten a good look at the van itself and was able to provide police with more details, including the fact that the van had had Minnesota license plates.

While police were now convinced that the van seen on the Oregon State University was the van used in Wilberger's abduction, they still had no idea where to find the van, and no idea who had been driving it. By November, 2004, six months after Brooke's abduction, investigators assigned to the case were still on square one. Little did they know though, that another crime was about to be committed in Albuquerque, New Mexico, and this crime would lead them right to Wilberger's killer.

Chapter 5

On November 29, 2004, a 22-year-old Russian exchange student, who goes by the pseudonym Natalie Kirov, left the daycare she worked at on the University of New Mexico campus for home. Minutes away from her doorstep, a car pulled up next to her and a man jumped out and told her to get into the car. Terrified, she complied.

The man held Kirov captive in his car at knifepoint as he drove off. When they got to a secluded area of a dead end road, the man pulled the car over and began to sexually assault the young woman, forcing her to remove her clothes in the process.

After sexually assaulting the Russian beauty, the man declared that he needed a drug fix, a "pick-me-up," and drove to a shady apartment complex to purchase some crack. He left Kirov in his car, bound up with her own shoelaces. While her captor was inside, Kirov managed to free her hands and unlock the car. She immediately ran into the street, despite being mostly naked, and flagged down a passing car.

Just as Kirov settles into the car she flagged down her captor emerged from the nearby apartment. After seeing how terrified Kirov became, her saviours quickly drove off in the opposite direction and brought her to the police station. She was finally safe.

Police immediately responded to Kirov's report by visiting the apartments her attacker stopped in to buy his drugs. They were able to find a lady willing to admit that a guy named Joel matching Kirov's description had stopped by earlier that night. Further, she knew where Joel lived.

Police immediately proceeded to the address given to them and immediately spotted the red car Kirov described parked in the lot outside. Police had just begun examining the vehicle when they were approached by a man who said he owned the car. Police asked him if his name was Joel, and he immediately responded yes. Police responded in turn by arresting him.

The Joel police now had in custody was Joel Courtney—a 38-year-old mechanic fisherman. Joel lived in Albuquerque with his wife and three children, but his marriage was incredibly unstable. Only a few weeks before this arrest, Courtney's wife had taken out a restraining order on him.

When police dug deeper into Courtney's past, they discovered that he had a long standing drug problem that they were able to trace back to his childhood in Beaverton, Oregon. Courtney had grown up an average, loving family, but his life began deteriorating after he started using drugs at the tender age of 11. By the age of 14, Courtney began repeatedly molesting his sister and cousins, and by the age of 19, he began experimenting with satanism, and was arrested several times for sexual assaults.

Now, many years later, he was back in custody for the sexual assault of Natalie Kirov, but it had been almost 20 years since he had been committed a crime, something Albuquerque detectives were skeptical of. They wondered if he had victimized any other women who crossed his path over the years, so they contacted authorities in Oregon, Courtney's home state, to ask if there were any unsolved crimes that matched Courtney's modis operandi. Almost immediately, Oregon police mentioned the disappearance of Brooke Wilberger six months ago, hoping to finally provide some answers to Wilberger's family and the surrounding communities.

Chapter 6

After having Joel Courtney brought to their attention, the Brooke Wilberger taskforce in Corvallis, Oregon decided to look further into Courtney's past to see if they could connect him to Wilberger's disappearance. They were quickly rewarded for this decision.

Investigators soon found out that Courtney and his wife had only recently moved to Albuquerque, New Mexico. Before that, the couple moved around Oregon frequently looking for cheap accommodations. At the time of Wilberger's disappearance, the couple were living with relatives in Portland, Oregon, an hour's drive away from Corvallis.

Further, investigators found that Courtney had been working for a janitorial company in Corvallis while he lived in Portland. He drove the company's 1997 green Dodge Caravan with Minnesota license plates to and from work each day.

Courtney's van was the exact van police had been trying to track down for the last several months. Armed with this knowledge, police managed to track down the vehicle, which was immediately brought to Portland to be searched for any forensic evidence that may have survived. Specifically, they were looking for any DNA evidence to compare to known samples of Brooke Wilberger and Joel Courtney himself.

While investigators waited for the DNA results to come back from the lab, they looked into Courtney's whereabouts the day Brooke Wilberger disappeared. They discovered that Joel Courtney had actually been expected in court to face a DUI charge that very day.

Police learned that on this day Courtney apparently made a call from Corvallis saying he would be late for his court time, but he never appeared. Police also learned that the next day, a disheveled Courtney had shown up at a family member's house 16-hours away from Corvallis. When asked why he was in such a state, Courtney came up with a story of how he ran into a gang of men in the woods who had captured a young woman and forced him to do terrible things he did not want to do. Amazingly, the family member chalked the unbelievable story to Courtney's chronic drug use, and never asked about it again.

On the one-year anniversary of Brooke Wilberger's disappearance, Corvallis investigators finally received the results of the forensic sweep of the green Dodge Caravan. It was worth the wait.

The evidence recovered from the van conclusively proved that not only had both Brooke Wilberger and Joel Courtney been in the green van, but Joel Courtney had been the person to place Wilberger there, and he likely knew where she was now. The final challenge investigators now had was getting Courtney to reveal this information so they could finally bring Brooke home.

Chapter 7

On August 2, 2005, Joel Courtney, who is preparing to go on trial for the kidnap and sexual assault of Natalie Kirov is served an arrest warrant for the kidnap and presumptive murder of Brooke Wilberger. Weeks later, the Kirov case is brought to trial, and faced with the indisputable evidence against him, Courtney pleaded guilty. He was given a sentence of 18 years in prison.

But Joel Courtney didn't have long to get settled in the New Mexico prison system. In April of 2008, he was extradited to Oregon in order to stand on trial for the charges laid against him in Brooke Wilberger's case.

When the trial began in Spring of 2009, the prosecutors in the case showed the court Joel Courtney's long standing history of sexual assaults against women, which dated back to his late teen years. They also presented a witness that had seen Courtney the night before Wilberger's abduction. This individual stated that they used to work together, and that they had spent the night of May 23, 2004, drinking and smoking crack together.

Although prosecutors had a large amount of evidence against Courtney, they were missing something very important, something desired not only by them but also by Wilberger's family and the entire community of Corvallis and Eugene—Brooke.

Up to this point, investigators had been unable to find any indication of Brooke's final resting place, and Courtney wasn't about to give this information up easily. The Wilberger family was all but begging the prosecutors and investigators working on Brooke's case to make a deal with Courtney so they could bring their daughter home and give her a peaceful burial.

The District Attorney eventually succumbed to the Wilbergers' wishes and presented a plea deal to Joel Courtney. The terms of the plea deal stated that Courtney needed to plead guilty to all charges against him and reveal the location of Brooke's remains. In exchange, Courtney would receive life in prison without parole.

Courtney rejected this initial offer, but quickly returned to the bargaining table. Courtney offered to plead guilty to the crime if he could be locked up in New Mexico near his family instead of in Oregon. He also promised to reveal the location of Brooke Wilberger's remains. Courtney's counter-offer was accepted and signed.

To uphold his side of the plea deal, Joel Courtney drew a map to Brooke's burial site for investigators and walked them through the events of May 24, 2004. He told investigators the story of how he forced the young woman into his van and took her to some nearby woods to sexually assault her. After being raped, Wilberger became enraged, and tried to fight her way to freedom. Courtney responded by punching Wilberger until she fell unconscious before beating her to her certain death with a piece of wood he found nearby.

Based on this confession, and armed with Courtney's map, investigators drove 10 miles outside of Corvallis to a heavily wooded area known as the Coast Range. Their goal: to locate Brooke's remains.

After several days of searching, investigators were finally able to locate Brooke Wilberger's remains in a shallow grave next to a clearing of trees. Her grave was hidden beneath a mound of tree branches and leaves. For the Wilbergers, the news was bittersweet. They finally knew what happened to their daughter, and they finally could bring her home, but up until this point they had always maintained hope that when she came home she would still be alive.

Joel Courtney was formally sentenced to life in prison without parole two months later, and was brought back to a New Mexico prison where he prepared to spend the rest of his days. It was the end of a violent sexual predator's freedom, but most importantly, it was the end of the mystery that had plagued Oregon police and Brooke Wilberger's friends and family for years.

Brooke was finally home and at peace, and the world was a little safer now with Joel Courtney now behind bars. This is little solace to those who continue to miss Brooke Wilberger dearly, but having some answers is inarguably better than none. Those who knew Brooke in life remember her as the sweet, caring angel she was. She had a good soul in her heart and a good head on her shoulders and would have undoubtedly achieved great things in life.

Brooke's family still keep in contact with the investigators that dedicated their time to bringing Brooke home—they attend the officers' retirement parties and exchange the occasional email—a small token of the gratitude they will always hold.

THE KIDNAPPING OF BOBBY GREENLEASE

NATHAN NIXON

The Bobby Greenlease Kidnapping

The story of Bobby Greenlease is that of a tragedy. This young boy was taken from the one place a child should always feel safe; a school. The heart of the collective world was shattered while witnessing the terrible, sickening events that were unfolding. Only monsters could do such terrible things. Who would do this? How could someone stoop to this level? Most importantly, why would someone resort to this? In 1950's rural America, crimes like this just didn't happen. The turmoil that would ensue after this horrible act is one of confusion, betrayal, and heart sinking results. An innocent boy was gone much too soon, and two senseless criminals were gone much too late.

The day was September 28, 1953. A school for small children in Kansas City, Missouri was having a normal day. Classrooms were filled with young children learning the basics for their futures. Children filed in by the dozens, eagerly greeted by the smiling, caring faces of the teachers they all had learned to trust and love. This was the essence of the French Institute of Notre Dame De Sion. This was the place of learning for six year old Bobby Greenlease.

In 1953, the level of school security was vastly lower than it is today. Teachers and administration alike were much more trusting of the adults that would interact on a daily basis with children. When a mysterious woman came through the front door of the school at 10:55 A.M. that morning, there was little more than a few questions of her intentions. This mystery woman explained that she was there to pick up Robert Cosgrove Greenlease Jr. In the routine of any school, teachers and office personnel quickly learn the family and caregivers of each of their students. Needless to say, there was some suspicion of this woman who had never before been through the doors of this school and most certainly had never had any interactions with Bobby Greenlease.

The mystery woman was very anxious. She was described later as "fidgety and nervous" by school personnel. She told them that the situation was dire. She explained that she was Bobby's aunt and that his mother had suffered a catastrophic heart attack. Bobby's mother was in the hospital and he needed to come with her at once. While the school personnel were quite suspicious, it was Bobby who quelled their worry. Bobby was pulled from class at approximately 11:05 A.M. and brought to the front of the school. The mystery woman got down on a knee in front of Bobby and quickly explained that he needed to come with her.

The innocence of Bobby Greenlease is ultimately what this woman was able to take advantage of. Bobby was a trusting little boy. He learned from his daily interactions to listen to the adults around him. His parents would later explain how he was such an easygoing little boy who never gave them problems. He was described by his teacher as happy and always striving to please. For Bobby, when an adult told him to do something, he did it. He trusted them, and he had learned at a young age that he was to do as he was told. Little Bobby Greenlease always did what he was told, and he always did it with a beautiful, contagious smile on his face.

Bobby took the hand of this mysterious woman quickly after she explained what had happened. The worries of school personnel were quelled by seeing the reaction of Bobby. Surely, they thought, he wouldn't seem so eager to go with this woman if he didn't know her. With that, Bobby Greenlease left the French Institute of Notre Dame De Sion with his "aunt." Sister Moreland later recalled that "Bobby went to her with no hesitation. As they walked out of the front door, she had one arm around his shoulder and the other one holding his hand. They entered into an awaiting taxi cab. Bobby showed no fear or withdrawal from her. Everything appeared as normal."

At around 11:30 A.M. a school official, Sister Marthanna, called the Greenlease home to learn the condition of Mrs. Greenlease. To her surprise, Mrs. Greenlease answered the phone. The conversation quickly alerted the school that the story was false. Mrs. Greenlease was terrified and immediately called her husband, Robert Cosgrove Greenlease Sr. As he rushed home from work, Mrs. Greenlease alerted the Kansas City police chief. The police chief alerted the FBI of the matter. In the span of just thirty minutes, it was clear that little Bobby Greenlease, full trusting and carrying the innocence that any six year old boy would, had been kidnapped by a mystery woman. A tragedy of epic proportions was unfolding. The events of this day would go on to grip the nation in a sickening, winding road of horror and greed. The investigation was on. The Greenlease family would not have to wait long for answers.

Being as the woman who had left with Bobby had entered a cab, the first job of investigators was to track down the cab driver. Later in the day, police tracked down Willard Pearson Creech. He was a cab driver working for the Toedman Cab Company of Kansas City, Missouri. He was fully compliant with police. He informed investigators that just before 11:00 A.M. a woman entered into his cab asking to be taken to the French Institute of Notre Dame De Sion. The description Creech gave fit that of the woman who had taken Bobby Greenlease. Before the woman exited the cab, she instructed Creech to wait for her outside the school. She had said that she also needed to be taken to the Katz Drug Store at Main and Westport in Kansas City. According to Willard, it was approximately 11 minutes later that the woman came out of the school with the young boy. The boy fit the description of Bobby Greenlease. The last time that Willard Pearson Creech saw the pair, they had stopped in the rear of an early 1950's blue Sedan with Kansas license plates.

The question that was being asked by everyone was why? Why would someone kidnap an innocent six year old boy? How could someone take a child from their school? These questions would be answered very quickly. What happens next sends a chill throughout the Greenlease household.

The first ransom letter arrives just hours after the kidnapping of Bobby. The Greenleases received a letter that was postmarked 6:00 P.M. and designated for special delivery. The letter made the intentions of the kidnappers apparent. The letter stated the demand of $600,000 to be placed in a duffle bag with no bills larger than $20. The ransom would be the largest, for that time, in the history of the United States. The kidnappers ended the letter by promising the safe return of Bobby Greenlease within just 24 hours. This was contingent upon receiving all of the demanded ransom money with no sneaky tricks attempted by investigators. This was the first of many ransom contacts by the kidnappers. Investigators say they received as many as six ransom letters and 15 phone calls. The next ransom letter, however, proved to be even more chilling than the first.

The next communication between the kidnappers and the Greenleases was a letter sent on September 29, 1953. It was postmarked 9:30 P.M. and again sent special delivery. The letter, however, accompanied the Jerusalem medal of which Bobby always wore. This terrified Bobby's parents. The letter again called for $600,000 to be given for the safe return of little Bobby. The kidnappers said that "Bobby was safe, but was becoming quite homesick and wanted to see his mommy."

Within days, the story of Bobby Greenlease had attracted national media attention. The nation collectively shared the grief of the Greenlease family and hoped wholeheartedly for the safe return of Bobby. People could not understand how someone could bring themselves to take a little boy from his school. Moreover, people could not wrap their minds around how the school could let this happen. How could a six year old boy be allowed to leave with a stranger of which the school had never seen before? Many more questions would be asked. The frightening answers would soon rise to the forefront of an investigation that had only just begun.

The final communication from the kidnappers was a phone call at 1:00 A.M. on October 5, 1953. The call came directly to the Greenlease residence. The kidnappers assured the family that Bobby was safe. They stated that they had received the ransom money and that Bobby would be released within 24 hours. This was the last time that the Greenleases would hear any correspondence from the kidnappers.

Carl Hall and Bonnie Heady never had any intentions to return Bobby Greenlease to his family. The grim details of the events that took place would soon be uncovered.

Bonnie Heady was they "mystery woman" who took Bobby Greenlease from Notre Dame De Sion. She had taken Bobby, by taxi, for a few miles where they would meet up with Carl Austin Hall. Bonnie and Bobby would get into a Plymouth station wagon with Carl where they traveled to Johnson County, Kansas. It was here where authorities say Carl Hall shot little Bobby Greenlease to death with a Smith and Wesson .38 caliber revolver.

Robert Cosgrove Greenlease Sr. paid the ransom money in full to the kidnappers. They were completely unaware that Bobby had been murdered on the day of the abduction. At the time, the $600,000 was the largest ransom ever paid in the United States. Upon receiving the ransom money, Carl Hall and Bonnie Heady drove 380 miles to St. Louis, Missouri. Hall became extremely paranoid all the while. He was certain that authorities were closing in on them. He decided to try to divert attention away from the area.

On October 5, Hall purchased a pair of metal suitcases to store the ransom money. He left the duffle bag in an ash pit near St. Louis. Hall had an apartment he had rented in St. Louis on Arsenal Street. In the late hours of October 5, Carl and Bonnie arrived at the apartment.

It is important to note that Bonnie Heady and Carl Hall were heavy drug and alcohol abusers. While not the only motive for the crime, it would explain the unthinkable acts committed by the pair of criminals. Bonnie Heady was a heavy heroin user. Carl Hall would take advantage of this for his own attempted escape.

When Hall and Heady arrived at his apartment, Bonnie was heavily intoxicated. Within minutes, she had fallen asleep in the apartment. This was exactly what Carl had wanted to happen. As soon as she was asleep, Carl took the ransom money and left. He had left his accomplice to the murder of Bobby Greenlease with just $2,000 of the ransom money. He placed the money in her purse and bolted out of the door. The pair had separated on October 5, 1953.

On October 6, Hall went to a local hardware store where he purchased two garbage cans and a shovel. Growing increasingly suspicious of authorities finding out who he was and tracking him down, he acquired a rental car that morning. He drove to the Meramec River in St. Louis County and anxiously looked for a suitable place to bury the ransom money. This proved unsuccessful. He ditched the empty garbage cans and made his way back to the Coral Courts Motel, where he had been staying. By this time the paranoia of Hall was destroying his mind. He became suspicious of other motel patrons that afternoon, and decided to leave the hotel and get a room at the Townhouse Hotel in St. Louis. This would prove costly.

On the afternoon of October 6 at approximately 3:30 P.M. St. Louis police received a call from John Oliver Hager. Hager was a driver for the Ace Cab Company in St. Louis. His information led to the arrest of Carl Hall on the evening of October 6, 1953 at the Townhouse Hotel where he had checked in earlier in the day. Had Hall stayed put at the Coral Courts Motel, he may have never been discovered by Hager. When police arrested Hall, he told them that his name was John James Byrne. This was obviously fictional, but perhaps was a last gasp for freedom. Later on that evening, Hall led police to Arsenal Street to his apartment where Bonnie Heady was staying. Police entered the residence in the late hours of October 6 and arrested Heady. The pair of kidnappers were in police custody.

This began a process of interrogations by the FBI. Hall was interrogated numerous times and put together an illustration of his involvement in the crime. He insisted that all of the $600,000 ransom money was in his possession. Carl Hall admitted to several allegations against him. He admitted to his part in the kidnapping of Bobby.

He admitted to actually planning and executing the kidnapping. He also admitted to burying the body of Bobby Greenlease on Heady's property. He even admitted to picking up the ransom money that was set in the requested duffle bag. He did not, however, admit to the actual killing of Bobby Greenlease. This, as he claimed, was carried out by one Tom Marsh.

Carl Hall described a grand scheme that he agreed to with a man named Tom Marsh. He described that, once he and Heady kidnapped Bobby Greenlease, they had given the boy over to Tom Marsh. The couple was to act as the "middle men" in a scheme to extort money from Robert Cosgrove Greenlease Sr. Carl Hall argued that Tom Marsh had killed Bobby, and it was only then that he agreed to bury the body in the shallow grave by the porch of Bonnie Heady's house. The investigators didn't buy it. After more interrogation, Carl reluctantly admitted that he and Bonnie Heady were the only involved parties in the kidnapping and subsequent murder of Bobby Greenlease.

The body of Bobby Greenlease was discovered by police the next day, October 7th, 1953 at 1201 South 38th Street in St. Joseph, Missouri. At approximately 8:40 A.M. police quickly came across the shallow grave while investigating the residence of Bonnie Heady. The body was discovered buried near the front corner of the porch. The little boy's body was wrapped in plastic bags and covered in lime. The Greenlease requested their dentist to positively identify the body. At 1:05 P.M. on October 7, it was officially determined by DNA and dental records to be the body of Robert Cosgrove Greenlease Jr. Bobby's body had been found.

Upon full examination of the house, investigators found heavy blood stains on the basement floor as well as the steps entering the Heady house. Blood stains were also found on two separate fiber rugs as well as a nylon blouse. This gave the indication to police that the body had been moved several times. In addition to the blood stains, several .38 caliber shell casings were found in the house. The FBI criminal investigation lab, after much testing, determined the casings had been fired from a .38 caliber snub nose Smith and Wesson revolver. This same revolver had been found in Carl Hall's possession at the time of his arrest. FBI investigators also determined that a lead bullet found in the floor board of a Plymouth station wagon owned by Bonnie Heady was also fired from the same revolver. They now had hard evidence, along with a near full confession, to indict Carl Hall and Bonnie Heady for the murder of Bobby Greenlease.

It was not until October 11, 1953 that the full story would come out. Carl Hall told investigators the events of Bobby Greenleases murder in full, gruesome detail. He explained that he and Bonnie Heady had taken the victim from Kansas City, Missouri to Overland Park, Kansas. This, he said, was the same day that they had kidnapped Bobby from school. It was a town just outside Kansas City. This is the location where Carl Hall murdered six year old Bobby Greenlease by firing multiple rounds from his .38 caliber Smith and Wesson revolver into the child. Carl Hall then explained that they then transported the body of Bobby 45 minutes away to St. Joseph, Missouri. He then buried the body near the porch in a shallow grave and proceeded to plant flowers on it.

Bonnie Heady subsequently admitted to assisting Carl Hall with the ransom letters. She admitted to providing the instructions of the ransom money drop off to the Greenlease family. She also admitted to being the "mystery woman" who picked up Bobby Greenlease from school on the morning of September 28, 1953. She told investigators of the ruse that she had planned to use to convince school officials into letting her have Bobby.

Carl Hall and Bonnie Heady were tried on October 30, 1953. This was just over a month after their kidnapping and murder of Bobby Greenlease. Judge Albert L. Reeves presided over the case in federal court in St. Louis, Missouri. Both Hall and Heady entered guilty pleas. Shortly after, on November 19, 1953, the jury deliberated for just one hour and eight minutes. They had heard all of the gruesome details of the case. By this time, the nation was gripped on the case. Each day, updates would be put in each city newspaper. Everyone was engulfed in the proceedings. When testimony came out that the couple had planned this disgusting act well in advance, the nation's collective voice screamed for the death penalty. On November 19, 1953, both Carl Hall and Bonnie Heady were recommended for the death penalty by the jury. After just 15 minutes of deliberation by Judge Reeves, he agreed that death by execution fit the crime. Judge Reeves sentenced them both to be executed on December 18, 1953.

"I think the verdict fits the crime," Judge Reeves said. "It is the most coldblooded, brutal murder I have ever tried."

On December 18, 1953, Carl Hall and Bonnie Heady were set to die in the Missouri State Penitentiary in Jefferson City, Missouri. They were executed in the gas chamber. Less than three months after the kidnapping and murder of Bobby Greenlease, Carl Hall was pronounced dead at 12:12 A.M. and Bonnie Heady was pronounced dead just 20 seconds later. A case that gripped a nation was now officially closed.

Officially, only half of the $600,000 ransom was recovered by authorities. In the weeks following the execution, the next step for investigators was to locate the rest of the ransom money. It was determined that the two suitcases which contained the other half of the ransom money were never brought in to the police headquarters at the time of the arrest. While lacking any evidence, the state decided to pursue charges against Lieutenant Louis Ira Shoulders and Patrolman Elmer Dolan. Shoulders was found guilty on April 15, 1954 and subsequently sentenced to three years in federal prison. Elmer Dolan was tried on March 31, 1954. He was also found guilty and sentenced to two years in federal prison. Both men were convicted of perjury. Both men served their sentences, after which they returned to the St. Louis area. Lieutenant Louis Ira Shoulders passed away on May 12,

1962, never having the mistake reconciled. Elmer Dolan was officially pardoned by President Lyndon B. Johnson on July 21, 1965. The lack of evidence against these two men was overlooked, most likely due to circumstance and the relentless effort by the investigation teams to close the case.

The mysterious disappearance of the ransom money has been the source of many myths and conspiracies. To the day, the ransom money has never been recovered. Investigation into a number of conspiracies and theories has turned up no trace of evidence to support them. Perhaps to understand the crime, we must understand who Carl Hall and Bonnie Heady were. To go through with such a horrific act, these two people must have been psychopathic in nature. Their story is one of wonder and disgust, most easily understood by looking at the mental make-up of each and how their paths crossed.

Carl Hall enjoyed great wealth in his childhood. He was the son of a prestigious and wealthy St. Louis lawyer. Hall never had to do any real work for a living. His father passed in 1946, leaving a fortune of $200,000 to his son. Ironically, it was through a heavy drinking habit and drug addiction that he quickly squandered his entire fortune. This would mark the beginning of a downhill spiral for Carl Hall.

Carl Hall had wasted a massive fortune. His drug and alcohol addictions, however, still remained. Upon losing his money, he set out to robbing innocent taxi cab drivers. The epitome of a "five dollars at a time" living, his take was said to be $38 at the time of his capture. He was found guilty of robbery and served 16 months in a state prison, and was released on April 24, 1953. This was a mere five months before his participation in the kidnapping of Bobby Greenlease.

While serving his 16 month sentence at Missouri State Prison, Hall began planning the kidnapping and murder of six year old boy Bobby Greenlease. Bobby was the son of the wealthiest man in Kansas City, Missouri. Robert Cosgrove Greenlease Sr. had gained great wealth as a car dealer. He had gained the bulk of his fortune by introduction

General Motors vehicles to the Midwest. The 71 year old also had some family ties to Carl Hall.

As a child, Carl Hall attended military school at the same location as the adopted step-brother of Bobby Greenlease. While they were not friends nor did they even speak to each other, the knowledge of the family was bestowed upon Carl Hall. This would be one more thing to solidify the target of Hall and Heady.

On April 24, 1953, Carl Hall stepped out of prison. He was immediately embraced by a strange woman of whom he had never met before. This woman was Bonnie Brown Heady. She was 41 years old at the time and recently widowed. She was described as a plump, pale woman with a "porcine" face. The mysterious woman kissed Hall on the mouth and held him close. Only after her passionate kissing did she introduce herself to Hall.

Bonnie Brown Heady was a gun smuggler in the 1930's. It was in this line of work she met a bank robber named Dan Heady. Dan was a smuggler, bank robber, and overall low grade criminal of the late 1920's to the 1930's. Dan married Bonnie in 1935. It wasn't long until Dan was arrested for numerous crimes. He attempted to escape from prison to get to his young, red-headed wife Bonnie. He was gunned down by a group of sheriffs before he could fully escape. The story told by the sheriff who shot Dan Heady is a chilling insight into the kind of person that Bonnie was. Upon learning of the shooting and subsequent death of her husband, Bonnie was described as saying "well that's too bad" out of the side of a sly, almost happy grin. It was the lifestyle that Bonnie craved. She was attracted to criminals.

She had heard about who Carl Hall was and the life he lived through many ex-prisoners. She was intrigued. She was addicted to men like Carl Hall and Dan Heady. She was also addicted to heroin and was a heavy alcohol abuser, much like Hall. Upon introduction herself to Carl Hall, she took him to her home in St. Joseph, Missouri.

This would prove to be a grim foreshadowing of the events that would take place just over five months down the road.

It is well known that Bonnie Heady was a heavy drinker and heroin addict. Carl Hall was just as guilty as Bonnie was in this regard. They would spend nearly every waking day drinking themselves into a stupor together. When they weren't too drunk to function, they would near overdose on heroin with one another. This engulfed their lives in the 5 months after they had met. This was how they lived their life in Bonnie's home in St. Joseph, Missouri.

It was in the few sober times together that they began to plan the horrific crime they would soon carry out. While Hall had planned out most of the major details while in prison, Heady helped with the finer points of how they would work the ransom and different ways to obtain the ransom without being seen by authorities. When Carl Hall originally proposed she be an accomplice in his terrible plan, Bonnie famously remarked, "Why, that's better than sex!" She had fully agreed to participate.

The night before the duo carried out their kidnapping of Bobby Greenlease, the actions they took part in were a sickening omen. These events were focused on closely in court, as it proved that this was not only a pre-meditated kidnapping, but more importantly it was a pre-meditated murder.

It was pouring down rain the night of September 27, 1953. The couple, wearing heavy boots and rain coats, dug the shallow grave just outside the porch of Bonnie's St. Joseph home. This was the critical piece that allowed jurors to swiftly come to a death sentence after just an hour of deliberation.

The personality that Bonnie Heady and Carl Hall had was on full display in their ransom calls with the Greenleases. The following transcript is one of many, but shows a pattern of the mental games that Hall and Heady were playing with the Greenleases. In the transcript, Hall identifies himself as "M."

Mrs. Greenlease: Hello, this is Mrs. Greenlease.

M: M speaking.

Mrs. Greenlease: We have the money, but we must know that our son is alive and doing well. Could you at least give me that? Can't you give me something that will assure that?

M: That is a reasonable request. To be completely frank with you, this boy is driving us nuts. We couldn't possibly risk taking him to a phone.

Mrs. Greenlease: Well, I can only imagine. Can you do this then? Can you ask him two questions? Give me the answer to the two questions.

M: Well.

Mrs. Greenlease: If I had the answer to these two questions, I would trust and know that my son is alive and well.

M: All right.

Mrs. Greenlease: Ask him the name of our driver in Europe from this summer.

M: All right.

Mrs. Greenlease: The second question is what did you build with the monkey blocks in your playroom the last night you were home with us? If you can get those answers for me, I will feel better and relieved. You know that is the only thing that I want.

M: We have the boy. He is alive and well. Believe me. He is literally driving us crazy.

Mrs. Greenlease: Well I can imagine that. He is a very active little boy.

M: He has been driving us crazy.

Mrs. Greenlease: Could you please get those answers from him?

M: All right.

Bonnie and Carl delighted in these phone calls. The duo deliberately extended the negotiations. They would make several, as many as 15, brief phone calls. Each call would change the plans for the ransom in a way that would extend the process another day. The sadistic cat and mouse game that Hall and Heady were playing with the Greenleases was absolutely sickening. The process was also delayed, moreover, due to the drunkenness of the kidnappers.

Another crucial bit of information was the confession that Carl Hall made about the night he killed Bobby Greenlease. Hall said that he sent Bonnie to take a walk in the field so she didn't have to witness the killing, as well as to keep an eye out for witnesses. It was then that Hall tried to strangle the young boy to death. Even for a six year old boy, Hall said that Bobby was providing strong resistance to this. He was fighting for his life. This actual court record confession from Carl Hall is both chilling and heart breaking.

"I was prepared for that. I had the gun in my coat pocket," Hall said. "I pulled it out and shot once, trying to shoot him in the heart. I had no idea if I had hit him or not, for he was still alive. I shot him through the head on the second shot. I then took him out of the car and laid him there on the ground. I had a plastic bag that I put him in. I remember there being a lot of blood there. This farm, where the killing occurred, is about two miles south and two miles west of the state line."

"I then called on Bonnie to return to the car," Hall continued. "She walked back to the car and help me load the body in the trunk. We drove straight back to her home in St. Joseph. We had to wait until night fall to bury the body; we didn't want the neighbors to see our movements and get suspicious."

When Judge Reeves announced the sentencing, the courtroom broke out into a tearful applause. "I'd rather be dead than poor," Bonnie Heady famously sneered after the sentence announcement. Robert Cosgrove Greenlease Sr. sat through the court proceeding quietly throughout the trial. In the most famous words spoken after the trial from the Greenlease family, he famously said "It's too good for them, but it's the best the law provides."

On September 28, 1953, an innocent boy was taken from his school by sick criminals. An innocent boy was murdered that night by these same sadistic people. Throughout the entire ordeal, the quest for money was a central force in the murder of Bobby Greenlease. Another force, however, was the crazy mental states of a duo of heroin addicts and alcohol abusers who enjoyed the lifestyle. When all was said and done, the entire nation had been taken on an emotional rollercoaster that, sadly, didn't have the happy ending that everyone was hoping for. Instead, a six year old boy was murdered and, although justice was done, it still didn't seem to be enough. For people to deem it a possibility to take a child from school, it doesn't seem that there would ever be a punishment fitting enough to provide the end that was due. From a kidnapping that started on the morning of September 28, 1953, to the gas chamber on December 18, 1953, Bonnie Heady and Carl Hall remained twisted and miserable. All that the Greenlease family could do was wonder what Bobby could have matured into being.